MOLDED ON A MOTORCYCLE

Wes Stephenson

Molded on a Motorcycle

A RIDER'S JOURNEY

eversity
Publishing

This book is dedicated to the fiery spirit of discovery and adventure, the pursuit of which can forge unbreakable bonds, one generation to the next. It is the author's deepest hope that this account will awaken and satisfy this spirit within each reader.

"From now on we live in a world where man has walked on the Moon. It's not a miracle; we just decided to go."

ASTRONAUT JIM LOVELL (GEMINI 7 AND 12;
APOLLO 8 AND 13)

CONTENTS

PREFACE

If you watch enough western movies, you will come across a term, usually directed toward the story's hero, "He sits a horse well." It means that the cowboy had a way of becoming one with his horse–the horse's movements were his own– both working together in perfect harmony. Not all who sit *on* a horse have learned to *sit* a horse.

The same can be true of a motorcyclist. Some ride *on* a motorcycle while some ride *with* the motorcycle, as flesh and iron combine into a single unit. The rider seems molded onto the bike. My Dad had this gift to a degree I've never seen matched. A few of my riding buddies have displayed the knack, and I've watched my sons evolve from being auxiliary attachments to their bikes to eventually becoming molded to their motorcycles.

But there is more to this "molded on a motorcycle" than the physical blending of man and machine. For me, the myriad of experiences and the people encountered while I have been on or around my motorcycles have formed the man I have become. To no small degree, I recognize that "Wes" would not be the same "Wes" had motorcycling not been such a large part of my life. Perhaps some other interest could have worked its way to a similar impact, but it would certainly not bring the same results. I sense that I would be a poorer man for the absence of my motorcycle and the worlds it has brought me to.

Motorcycling has sparked treasured friendships and built unbreakable bonds with loved ones. My bike has injected me with adrenaline through life-confirming thrills and settled my soul in wonder as, cresting a hill or rounding a curve, I discovered this incredibly palatial planet. Its saddle has been my mountain-top sanctuary for introspection. Our journeys have afforded me the time and the effective silence to allow wisdom to distill from contemplation. It has been my spiritual retreat, my Mount Sinai, where I've conversed with God and came away better directed and infused with hope.

I've experienced nothing inanimate possessing more soul than a motorcycle–nothing designed by man that better connects to things larger than man. Yet I don't consider my motorcycle a molten idol worthy of worship in and of itself. Instead, I see it as a steady and like-minded companion who, like Frodo's faithful comrade Sam in *The Lord of The Rings*, has carried me to rendezvous with greater actions, insights, and fulfillment than I would ever have encountered had I chosen to remain in the cottage.

The motorcycle. From tales and traditions that predate my birth– from its omnipresent influence throughout my childhood–from links forged to bind me to my father with a continued chain that is now fastened firm to my own posterity–from the scars I've earned and the lessons I've learned, I must gratefully acknowledge that I have been, and continue to be, molded on a motorcycle.

It is my sincerest hope that the pages of this book will deliver a good degree of *what it's like* to have lived the life of a motorcyclist. I hope that my experiences may, to some measure, become the reader's own, whether or not they will ever swing a leg over a motorcycle and hit the open highway.

PROLOGUE
MY FATHER'S FINAL GIFT

This is, I believe, the last photo taken of my father before his passing. Alzheimer's had claimed all but sparse fragments of his wonderful mind, and he had recently been admitted to a full-time care facility. With each visit, I sought for anything that he might find familiar so that we could have a "conversation" for at least a sentence or two. On this day, I rode over on my newly acquired Harley Davidson Springer Softail, and I was eager to see how Dad would react to an object he knew so well. Dad had gone through 37 Harleys over the years; from a war-surplus flat-head "eighty" he purchased as he mustered out of

WWII to his beloved "Big Red" Electra Glide Sport that he rode well into his late seventies.

As children, we pestered Dad to tell of his two-wheeled adventures of riding hard and fast with college buddies Bunkie Ramey, Gene Clampett, and "Cheeseburger" Smith, and we knew all the stories well. In a very real sense, my own motorcycle life began a decade before I was even born. Dad's stories were so frequently and vividly related that I could feel the wind, smell the freshly-Gunked engine, and hear the laughter as if the memories were my own. We showed our friends the trophy Dad won at a hill climb competition in Arkansas. He won it using the stock motorcycle that he rode to the event after no competitor was able to crest the hill during the first heat. We stared wide eyed, and frequently laughed to tears, at his tales of adventurous rides with Bob Hunt, a larger-than-life character and a lifelong friend, who rode with Dad for over 50 years.

"Slim" Stephenson (Dad) is the tall guy in center, surrounded by college riding buddies at University of Arkansas. On Dad's right is Sid Gray, owner of the Fayetteville, AR, Harley shop

| Dad scrambling through the woods on his Hydra-Glide

We took particular delight in hearing how in the mid-1950s, Dad's blue Harley Duo Glide blasted past a car driven by a young secretary who, upon arriving at work and spotting the motorcycle parked nearby, commented to her boss, "The maniac on that motorcycle is going to get himself killed!"

Her boss smiled and replied, "That would be Jim Stephenson, and you may be right; he might die on that *motorsickle*, but I'll bet he won't be getting hit from behind!"

My dad married that secretary, and Mom and Dad rode that motorcycle all over the U.S. and Mexico long before I was born.

Some of my earliest memories, from when I was little more than a toddler, include seeing the world through the windshield of a Harley as Dad sat me on the gas tank in front of him and tucked my feet behind his knees.

I was ten years old when he put me on the back of his '68 model for a ride from Kansas City, Missouri, to Cape Canaveral, Florida.

I was only fourteen when he and I rented two motorcycles in Athens, Greece, and toured the countryside, inadvertently getting ourselves into the middle of a Grand Prix automobile race (riding the wrong way on their circuit) and dealing with troubles from the local authorities.

I was just sixteen, with my signature still wet on my first driver's license, when Dad and I took a pair of motorcycles and my two younger brothers on a 7,000-mile tour of the United States. We camped next to our bikes and made memories that remain vivid even forty years later.

The intervening years had been full of new adventures with countless cross-country rides with Dad. We rode identical Electra Glides and viewed the world through matching lenses shaped by convictions and sensibilities harmonized in chats around a campfire and in laughter that echoed off the overpasses as we sheltered from a downpour to don our rain suits.

The day my dad and I took the picture at the beginning of this prologue, I entered his room and reintroduced myself, "Good morning, Dad. It's your favorite son, Wes. How are you doing?" All my siblings employed their own version of this salutation.

His eyes studied me with a guarded look as he protected himself from the strangers who seemed to fill his life anew each day. On most visits, after ten minutes or so of conversation, he would begin to use my name and become aware of our connection, though I was sometimes considered his son and at other times his brother.

"Hey, Dad. Let's find your shoes. I've got something outside that you're going to love."

I put his shoes on for him and guided him down the hall, repeatedly reminding him that we were going outside because I had a surprise for him. As we shuffled onto the driveway, his eyes widened upon spotting the big silver Harley.

I wish that I could report that Dad smiled when he saw the bike, but that facial expression was no longer part of his inventory by this time. Still, his eyes surveyed the Hog from stem to stern, accompanied with what appeared to me to be slight nods of approval. I encouraged him to swing a leg over the bike, and then I helped him to do so. His hands went immediately to the controls, and I could sense familiarity creeping in.

I asked him what he thought of the motorcycle, and he mumbled, "She's a *beaut*," as his head swiveled left and right to take everything in, but he didn't say anything more.

A nurse stepped out, and I asked her if she would shoot a photo of the two of us. I helped Dad dismount and we both leaned back on the Harley for one final picture from the saddle. We then started the slow walk across the driveway.

Ten feet from the motorcycle, Dad came to a halt and looked at me with his brow furrowed in thought.

"Do you really like that motorcycle, Wes?" he asked.

I told him that it was a real crackerjack.

He looked back at the Harley and shook his head as he bit on his bottom lip. When he looked back at me, tears welled in his eyes. "Then I want you to have it," he said, taking me by the arm and looking deep into my eyes.

My mouth opened, but I didn't know how to respond.

He again offered, but with increased resolution about the rightness of his decision. "She's yours… I want you to have it."

My father was *giving* me my own motorcycle, and for a fraction of a second, I thought it was humorous. But his eyes held mine, and I could see that Dad truly believed that this was his motorcycle. If it had ever been true that "it's the thought that counts," it could never have been truer than at that moment when thoughts were precious to begin with and time was running out on their continued exchange.

I gazed in awe into his watering eyes, and I *knew* that my dad loved me. He was a man who was aware of nothing remaining in his life to give but this motorcycle, and so his gift was one of totality; his offering was entire… Whole… Complete.

I simply thanked him for his most generous gift, and for the first time in quite a while, he seemed satisfied with the state of things around him.

It was a slow ride home that morning. The Harley pulled strong, but I kept the reins slack, more interested in contemplation than in exhilaration. I realized that I was experiencing a gift that was not just a figment of a confused imagination. The joy of riding was a gift from my father. The appreciation of things mechanical was a gift from my father. The ability to partake of the world as I passed through it was a gift from my father. The things that I have come to love; the faith that I have embraced; the values that guide my life are all gifts bestowed upon me, in large measure, by my wonderful father.

I pulled the Harley into my garage and shut it down. The motor ticked and popped as parts began to cool. Before entering the house, I looked back to the shiny silver steed.

My father's final gift?

No. It was one of his first–and it renews itself every day.

CHAPTER 1
JUST A FEW MORE MILES

Three o'clock in the morning and all is blackness. The sky, the earth, the blacktop. It's all just blackness, top to bottom.

My motorcycle headlight illuminated three recurring objects: the occasional exit sign; a slow and constant cadence of small green highway mile markers, and a continuous machine-gun burst of white highway stripes shooting by my left foot at a rate of three stripes per second. After 1000 miles and 23 hours in the saddle, I fought to stay awake. I felt the fading, and I sensed I had missed a moment of consciousness. I shook my head and checked my mirrors. Two head-lights, one close, one distant, trailed behind me. I chopped the throttle and motioned to the rider immediately behind me to pull alongside. My oldest son, Trent, came abreast, and I slapped my helmet, shook my head, and pointed at the next exit sign. He acknowledged with a nod and accelerated to take the lead.

Trent pulled off Interstate 84 at Exit 263–Juniper Road. No town. No gas. No services. No lights. Nobody.

Trent pulled his Harley Super Glide to a stop and dismounted. I brought the Beemer in close behind. My youngest son, Mitch, pulled his Intruder along flank. Trent shouted out to Mitch above the idling exhausts, "Dad's sleepy! How you doin'?"

We were southbound in the high desert of Idaho, just twelve miles from our target: the Utah state line. This small segment of our jour-ney–this relatively puny strip of tar–will bring to a completion our version of the Iron Butt 48-State Challenge: to ride our motorcycles through parts of all 48 of the lower US states within a ten-day riding window.

At Exit 263, we had covered over 8,000 miles and had two hours remaining on the clock to traverse these last dozen miles.

That's only ten minutes of riding, I told myself. *Ten minutes out of a lifetime of riding motorcycles.* But it was ten minutes longer than I could muscle my will to remain alert and to continue functioning.

I folded my arms across the handlebars, leaned forward, and laid my still-helmeted head onto the sleeves of my leather jacket. Mitch dismounted and did a few windmills to stretch and rejuvenate. Trent stepped behind me and massaged my shoulders. "Come on, Dad–," Trent said, "let's do a few wind-sprints–have another granola bar and down some Gatorade. That last hour was some boring riding, but we can get our juices going again. Come–run with me."

CHAPTER 2
GENESIS - BEFORE MY WORLD WAS

Infused with its essence, saturated by its spirit. Not just from the womb—before that. The motorcycle, in its romantic sense ("Marked by the imaginative or emotional appeal of what is heroic, adventurous, remote, mysterious, or idealized" –Webster), began to mold my life years before my first breaths. These iron steeds played a role in my creation and in my gestation: first, by introducing my parents to one another; then by adding the soothing rumbled rhythm as a lullaby while I incubated within my mother on the back seat of a Harley.

In the summer of 1957, I took my first long-distance motorcycle trip while secured safely within the womb as my folks rode from Kansas City, Missouri, to Veracruz, Mexico, in the company of their riding buddies, Bob and Maryann Hunt. As a matter of fact, it was on this trip that I was in my first motorcycle accident, six months before I was born. My dad told me the tale and it went something like this:

"You gotta know that Hunt was a competitive guy who didn't like being showed up in any way, particularly when it came to his *motor-sickle*. For example, on one of our first rides together, he and I overnighted in a cabin near Eureka Springs, Arkansas. The night was cold, and when we came out to our Harleys in the morning, ice caked our seats and windshields. The engine oil gets thick when things drop below freezing, so it was a challenge to get the motorcycles to kick over. We both stood on our kick starters and cycled them through again and again. They barely moved at first, but eventually, we were able to put some force into our kicks. I was able to get my sickle fired up, but Bob struggled. The harder he worked, the hotter he got– both physically and emotionally. The fact that my Hog was now idling just fine added to his anger. He peeled off his jacket and cussed as he continued to kick. Then he peeled off his outer shirt and wiped away sweat despite the low temperatures. Exhausted, he paused to catch his breath, and I asked him if he wanted me to give it a try. Convinced that I would fare no better, he stepped aside and waved his hand toward his bike. I went through the same routine I used for my motor, (half-choke, two twists of the throttle, and spark advanced). Bob's Hog fired up on my second kick.

"Hunt spit once on the ground then walked around to the front fender of his motorcycle. He balled up his fist and punched his Harley square in the windshield, which shattered in the cold, leaving an eight-inch hole in the center. I didn't dare say a word. We just mounted up and rode away with Hunt now dealing with an extra bit of chilled breeze coming at him from the center of his windshield.

"So," my father continued, "Understanding his temperament as a background, I'll tell you about our trip to Mexico.

"Me and your mom and Hunt and his wife headed off on our two Harleys for Veracruz in the summer of '57. Somewhere in Texas, Bob and Maryann were riding in front of us when they went down after hitting some gravel on a curve. I watched them slide out and was able to slow down to avoid the same fate. They both got skinned up a bit– nothing serious, and the bike's crashbars took most of the scrapes. By this time, I'd gotten to know Hunt quite well and was comfortable pushing his buttons. I asked his wife if she wanted to join Billye and me on my bike or if she was still comfortable riding with her husband. Hunt was steamed, but he could give as good as he got with a quick and biting wit. He looked for every opportunity to get a dig in at me, as few as those opportunities might have been.

"After entering Old Mexico, a portion of the ride passed through low mountains, I was in the lead. After a time, Hunt and I became separated; at least, I couldn't see him in my rearview mirror. Your mom and I came upon a slow-moving tanker truck in the twisties, and we fell in behind it. As the tanker negotiated the curve, my eye caught sight of something coming out of the top of the tanker, and by the time I realized that it was sloshing oil onto the road, it was too late. We went down on the curve, and your mother and I slid side-by-side as we watched the Harley spin on its side down the road in front of us.

When we came to a stop, we stood and brushed ourselves off. We hadn't been going very fast, we were wearing our leather jackets, and neither of us were hurt. We looked back up the road behind us and we didn't see the Hunts. We hurried to the motorcycle, got it upright, fired it back up, then continued on our way, relieved that we had not been caught having 'gone down.'

"We pulled over at a cantina just a mile or so later, parking the Harley out front so that Hunt would see where we had stopped. We made sure to keep the scratched side of the bike away from easy view. We went inside, hung our matching gray leather jackets on hooks near the table, and sat down to order lunch.

"About five minutes later, we heard Hunt's motor pull up, and shortly thereafter, Bob and Maryann joined us at the table. The lunch conversation went as usual, and we said nothing about our little spill. As we awaited our bill, Hunt's eyes became fixed on our jackets, hanging nearby. He glanced at me, then back to the jackets. I looked up at the jackets and noticed the scuff marks on the shoulders and backs. Hunt's eyes shifted back to me as a broad grin spread across his face.

"'You been down!' he offered through his still-grinning teeth. He chuckled and looked to his wife, 'They've been down, and they weren't going to tell us about it.'"

My dad summed up the episode with, "I don't think I could have gotten Hunt a greater gift than to have slid out my motorcycle on the same trip that he had dumped his."

I have since thought that there should be a scripture (there almost is) that would go something like this: *And greater love hath no man than this: That he lay down his motorcycle for his friends,"* (Harley 1:74).

And that was my first motorcycle mishap—as the "passenger within a passenger" on my folk's Harley in the hills of Old Mexico.

Somewhere in that last trimester, before my *zero-birthday*, I began the longest hiatus from motorcycle riding I would experience in my entire life; it was two and a half more years before Dad sat me on the gas tank of his Harley with my feet tucked tight behind his thighs and my hands reaching forward to grasp the center of the handlebars. It was then that I would again feel the rumble of his big twin motorcycle. I don't recall anything of life before the age of four, but by that age, I remember vying with my brothers for "tank time" with Dad as he motored us gently around the neighborhood.

Even though, as an adult, I would go on to negotiate curves at triple-digit speeds while grinding the footpegs into the pavement, I don't believe I have ever felt a greater sense of *leaning*–of feeling like the entire world was tipped on edge–than what I felt as a child astride the tank of Dad's Harley. When Dad hit second gear and cracked open the throttle, usually for only a moment, my head rocked back and bounced against my dad's chest–THAT was the thrill that grabs you by the spine and never lets loose. I've been chasing a similar thrill for sixty years.

I didn't start operating a motorcycle myself until I was eight years old, but by that time, I'd already amassed tens of thousands of *dry miles* from the saddle of my dad's *motorsickles* as they sat parked in our garage, my imagination guiding my Harley across the country.

Dad's Harley was a combination of monkey bars and time machine. Weighing in at 700 lb., the Electra Glide remained securely heeled over on its considerable kickstand even with a pair of us kids scrambling up the wrong side of the bike–at least, none of us ever came close to tipping one over. From that saddle I relived, in detail, every story we could pry out of Dad (and Mom). Each of us boys had our favorite tales, but one in particular led the list and became my go-to episode anytime I had the garage to myself.

I'd climb up on the buddy-seat and slide all the way forward to where the saddle perched above the rear portions of the dual fuel tanks. Leaning forward, I could rest one hand on the throttle grip, but my *wingspan* was not yet broad enough to grasp the other grip, so I rested it casually on the tank as if, "That's just how cool I am." I'd look out through the windshield, and in my mind, the garage walls would evaporate into the memorized description of a hot Arkansas day in 1953.

"So, we were riding along–just me and my buddy, Gene Clampett. We'd left Fayetteville that morning, heading for Shreveport on U.S. 71, riding matching Harley Hydra-Glides. By early afternoon, the sun began to bake the air so that even the breeze was not a relief. As we crested a hill, the two-lane highway dropped to reveal the countryside opening into a broad meadow below, still a half-mile away. To the right of the road, a large pond shimmered silver in the sunlight. I looked over at Clampett and he nodded–a quick swim would do us both some good on this sweat-sapping ride.

"We pulled the *sickles* over on a broad patch of dirt just off the highway and adjacent to the pond. There wasn't much traffic on 71, and we waited until there were no cars in sight in either direction. We peeled off our clothes for a quick skinny-dip in the pond. Checking for traffic one more time, we dashed to the shore and into the water. We ran ten yards– twenty yards– thirty yards. We ran to the center of the pond and found that nowhere was the water deeper than six inches! Our eyes shot to the crest of the hill, and we saw a semi-truck descending followed by a station wagon. We dove onto our bellies and searched for a deeper pocket of water. Another car appeared from the other direction as we wallowed like hogs in the mud with nothing but our heads, shoulders, and shiny white butts sticking out from the pond! We could do nothing but laugh and imagine what the motorists were thinking as they paraded by.

"After a few minutes, there was a break in traffic, and we made a dash for the sickles, hiding behind them as we scraped the mud from our bodies and slipped back into our denims and jackets. We were relieved that none of the passersby included a patrolman and that no one stopped for a chat."

Clampett takes a break during one of their rides.

My imagined Arkansas faded away and the garage walls reappeared as I slapped my faithful steed, thanking it for carrying me away on another escapade. I climbed down from the Harley to find my Schwinn, the one with the right-side hand grip loosened from being wrenched again and again in vain attempts to find power. On my Schwinn, I mimicked the adventures of my idols and their two-wheeled machines.

CHAPTER 3
A VISION TAKES SHAPE

Charlotte, North Carolina, Summer, 2015– I'm 57 years old, and in this latter half of my life, two quotes have echoed frequently in my ears. The first is a tragic refrain from a Bengali poet; a lamentation that I would dread to utter at life's closing:

"I have spent my days stringing and unstringing my instrument, while the song I came to sing remains unsung" – Rabindranath Tagore.

The second quote is from one of the world's most accomplished explorers and reveals the key to avoiding the aforementioned regrets:

"From now on we live in a world where man has walked on the Moon. It's not a miracle; we just decided to go" – Astronaut Jim Lovell (Gemini 7 and 12; Apollo 8 and 13).

I love those words, "We just decided to go…" We made a commitment, circled a date, and went to the Moon. Perhaps then, the most important tools for achieving our goals, ("Singing our song" as the poet might say), may be a wall calendar and a permanent marker. Just circle a date and decide to go. The decision to act becomes more important than all subsequent decisions because it is the one that made all the other decisions possible.

By the summer of 2015, I had grown sensitive to ambitions and dreams, whether my own or those of others, that were accompanied with wistful statements of "wouldn't it be nice"– "when I get some time"– "someday, when life settles down"–or the self-delusional, "I'm fixin' to…"

There was an adventure I'd had my eye on for many years, and I was feeling a desperate need for a calendar and an irrevocable decision. I was becoming more and more aware that my physical *prime time* was waning with each passing year and that tomorrow may not be soon enough for accomplishing tasks that require physical sharpness and vitality.

In the world of long-distance motorcycle riding, there are a few brass rings that represent the pinnacle of the sport: grueling rides requiring insightful preparation, solid equipment, stout physical endurance, and a fair measure of good fortune. Many of these challenging rides are specified, and their successful completion certified by an organization called The Iron Butt Association (yes, that really is the name). These certified rides include:

- The Saddlesore 1000 (riding 1000 miles in less than 24 hours)
- The Bumburner 1500 (riding 1500 miles in less than 36 hours)
- The 50CC (riding coast to coast in less than 50 hours)
- The 48 State Challenge (riding through all 48 of the lower US states within ten days)

This 48 State Challenge was my brass ring: only 240 hours allotted for touching my tires into every one of the contiguous states. There would be no mulligans allowed, no forgiveness for circumstances out of the rider's control. Bad weather? Too bad. Mechanical failures? Tough luck–deal with it on the spot and quickly. Finish in time or fail.

In the course of four decades, I had ridden on four continents and crisscrossed a great portion of the United States on many occasions. I could relate to my father's bold brag, "I've used more chain oil than most riders have used gasoline." Still, I wasn't acquainted with anyone who had completed the Iron Butt 48 State Challenge, and I wanted to attempt something more difficult than I was certain I could accomplish. I hoped to cap my life's passion (sports-wise) with this rarely accomplished feat. I took out the calendar, flipped forward two years, and circled the month of June 2017.

My riding experience led me to focus on the month of June to minimize the chances of weather blocking my progress. The high passes of the northern Rockies are generally clear of snow by then, and the Southwestern deserts would not yet have hit their summertime highs.

We'd be at the tail end of the spring tornado season in the Midwest, and hurricanes would not yet have begun to form along the Eastern Seaboard and Gulf Coast states. Once my dates were set, I'd have to deal with whatever weather challenges appeared, but an early summer time frame would improve my chances for avoiding catastrophic conditions.

To keep myself in check from backing out or postponing this adventure, I decided to make my intentions known to family, friends, and colleagues. My wife, who loves to perch on the seat behind me on more sedate rides, was fully supportive but made it clear that she wanted no part of something this torturous, and I was inwardly glad I didn't have to "disinvite" her. This would be tough enough to complete solo, and I didn't want even the minor delays of dealing with additional bio breaks or fatigue issues beyond my own.

Except for a few of my hard-core riding buddies, none of my friends had even heard of the 48 State Challenge, and they all seemed to agree that they would not want to attempt this circuit even in a car unless they had a month to do so. Of my fellow riders, a few initially expressed enthusiastic interest in joining my adventure, but the difficulties of getting a few weeks away from work and family caused them all to bow out. Perhaps too, (although never stated), the realization that this would be far from a pleasure ride played a role in their decisions to pass on this adventure. For whatever reasons, I soon saw that this was developing into what I had originally expected: one man, one machine, one continent.

However, a phone call from my oldest son, Trent, brought a welcome dynamic to the odyssey. He was dead set on joining me for the ride despite living on the opposite end of the country, currently having no motorcycle, and his tenure at his place of employment would make it difficult to accumulate enough vacation time for undertaking this journey. But once decided, Trent's mind was on rails, and we both knew this would be a father-and-son adventure destined to be a pinnacle point in our relationship.

Besides, I owed Trent an epic ride. When each of our six children (four daughters, two sons) graduated from high school they were granted a cross-country ride with Dad, complete with campouts under the stars and new horizons to reel in. Jill and I rode to the Grand Canyon and explored the mountain country of Arizona. Kim's trip was riding the Rockies of Colorado. Rachel joined me for a tour of the

Pacific Coast Highway and five western states. Audrey demanded to see Yellowstone and the high plains of Montana. Mitch and I took two bikes on a two-week 6000-mile ride from Utah to Illinois, and we captured part of Canada on our way home.

But Trent... Well, all our efforts to put together a decent ride seemed to be snake-bit. His "Graduation Ride" began as the two of us left our home in Las Vegas on two bikes, a Harley Electra Glide, (a.k.a. "Rumbling Red"), and a Suzuki Intruder 800. In northern Utah, I received an emergency phone call that forced us to abort the trip and return home to Vegas. Although Trent and I enjoyed several weekend rides together in the years since his graduation, his was still "the ride that got away," and the thought of having him accompany me on the 48-state odyssey seemed like the perfect thing to restore balance to our motorcycling universe.

Trent and I have always been close with many interests in common, including motorcycles, and as it was with my own father, motorcycles have played a role in creating some important teaching moments–sometimes for him and sometimes for me.

———

When Trent was seven years old, I was one day washing my Harley on the front lawn while Trent and his siblings were playing tag in the grass. Among my buckets, rags, and brushes, I had also brought out a couple of SOS scouring pads (steel wool infused with blue soap) to use in cleaning the thin whitewalls on the tires. I had been scrubbing away for ten minutes at the front wheel when I stood to get the hose for a rinse-off. It was then that I spotted Trent with a wet SOS pad in his hand. My eyes shot to the big red gas tank and saw that it was covered in blue suds. Without a thought, I shouted, "NOOO!" I snatched the scouring pad out of Trent's hands. With a pained voice, I scolded my boy, "NEVER use that on a painted surface – it'll scratch the HECK out of the tank!"

I turned the hose onto the tank, rinsed the suds away, and searched the finish to assess the damage. The Harley's resilient clearcoat and the meager pressure applied by a small boy's thin arm resulted in no significant damage. I turned to tell my son that no harm was done, but he was nowhere in sight.

An awareness settled upon me of the harshness of my reaction to my son's effort to help. I turned off the hose and went into the house to find Trent. As I walked the halls and called out his name, my better sense told me that my boy was only wanting to join with me, to be a part of what I was doing. Trent and I were best of buddies, and I knew that he knew that the Harley was one of my treasures. I was sure that he must be mortified to think he had hurt my motorcycle.

When there was no answer in the house, I walked out to the back yard. There, in a corner behind his wooden fort, Trent sat on the ground, hugging his knees. He raised a tear-streaked face at my approach, and a lump formed in my throat. I knelt and drew him into my arms. "I'm sorry, son. Everything is alright. The Harley is fine, and I was wrong to yell at you."

I carried him around to the front yard and right up to the Harley as his sniffles continued. I pointed to a bit of chrome on my right spotlight that showed some deep scoring. I asked him if he knew how that had happened. Trent's eyes refilled with tears as he lowered his head and responded, "I scratched it when I washed it."

"No," I replied, "You didn't scratch anything, Trent. I am the one who scratched this spotlight about a year ago, and do you know how I did it?"

His head raised to look me in the eyes, "No. How?"

"I was having a hard time getting some bugs off the chrome, and I thought that an SOS pad was softer than this metal and, therefore, wouldn't scratch it. I then scrubbed on the bugs, but when I rinsed away the suds, I saw that I had scratched the chrome. I made the very same mistake that you made, but mine left a mark while yours didn't."

He brightened, "YOU did that?"

I nodded, "Yep. I just didn't realize what that SOS pad would do. And you didn't either, did you?"

He shook his head as I sat him down on the saddle and I continued, "But even if yours HAD left scratches, I want you to know that you mean more to me than this motorcycle. I know you were just trying to help, and I'm very sorry for getting angry."

Trent and I resumed the washing of the Harley, but this time we used sponges and rags.

| Young Trent on one of my old BMWs, dreaming of roads ahead.

This 48 State Challenge would be, for Trent and me, the chance to take revenge on the fates that had kept that big father-son ride an ever-elusive dream. Once Trent became my partner in this, a new level of enthusiasm emerged as he and I swapped countless emails and phone calls discussing routing, equipment, and optimal dates for the adventure. We began to feel it - there was something about creating a blueprint that started to clothe the dream with substance.

CHAPTER 4
A THOUSAND-MILE TEST RUN

We both wished that Trent's younger brother, Mitch, could join us for the 48-state ride (such a threesome would be absolutely ideal), but Mitch had a young family and a new job, and he simply could not clear a way to be gone for so long a time. Ironically, Mitch was the only one of my two boys who then had a motorcycle.

We were still nearly two years out from the target date when Trent and I began emailing one another with proposed course routes. The Iron Butt Association did not prescribe, nor care, what states were the starting or finishing points, and we were free to choose whatever roads we felt would convey us to our waypoints the quickest. Their rules were simple:

- Have an independent witness certify your start time.
- Obtain a time-stamped and dated gas receipt with a printed address proving you were in each of the 48 states (even if barely over the state line).
- Complete the 48 states within 240 hours.
- Obtain an independent witness to certify your completion.

The course we mapped out would cover over 8000 miles, requiring a pace of more than 800 miles per day. Because we realized that we must plan on weather delays, road construction, and heavy congestion in certain regions of the country, some days would fall well short of the 800-mile target. This meant that we must be prepared to put in a few 1000-mile days to compensate. Those kinds of days would not be easy; after all, there is a reason that 1000-mile days come with their own certifications from the Iron Butt Association. To have to do a few of these within a single circuit would be extremely taxing.

I knew that Trent had taken many regional three-day rides but that he had never ridden more than 400 miles in a single day. Even in my decades of cross-continent riding, I had only accomplished a 1000-mile day twice, and I was 18 years old when I did my first one (Cape Canaveral, Florida, to St. Louis, Missouri). I was 19 when I did it the second time (Longview, Washington to Las Vegas, Nevada). But back in the mid '70s, there was no Iron Butt Association to certify those long rides, so I had always considered myself an "unofficial" member of the club.

As the Spring of 2016 approached, the thought of completing 1000-mile days was heavy on my mind. I was 58 years old and in good general condition, but I felt that I should probably test both myself and my equipment by taking a test run to officially earn my Saddlesore 1000 certificate from the Iron Butt folks. I searched Google Maps for destinations 500 miles by interstate from my home in Charlotte, and I selected a route to and from Louisville, Kentucky, for the round-trip single-day ride. I then circled another date on the calendar, choosing Saturday, May 14th for this attempt.

As the day approached, I serviced Big Red (my 1990 Harley Electra Glide), packed the saddlebags with *eat-em-as-you-ride* fare, such as beef jerky, granola bars, and string cheese. I checked the weather forecast, which called for dry roads and partly cloudy skies.

I left Charlotte at 5:15 Saturday morning, stopping first to get a time-and-date-stamped gas receipt that marked the official start of the ride. I needed to complete the 1000-mile circuit by 5:15 a.m. the next day.

The route was simple: ride north on I-77 into Virginia and into West Virginia, then catch I-64 bending west into Kentucky, eventually to Louisville. I had arranged to meet a friend who lived in Louisville, and he would be my witness that I reached the apex of the ride.

As I left Charlotte, the morning air was quite cool, but the leather chaps and heavy riding jacket kept me comfortable in the predawn darkness. While the exhaust gasses exited the motorcycle through the fishtail pipes at the rear, there was a very welcome aroma that wafted up from the big twin cylinder motor rumbling below me.

Like most kids in my neighborhood, my Saturday chores included such things as raking leaves and sweeping the driveway. From around the age of eight, I had one chore that was outside the norm for most boys: Dad would pull his Harley, along our small stable of Honda dirt bikes, onto the gravel behind the garage and assign me to Gunk the engines.

GUNK® is a brand of engine degreaser that is now sold in aerosol cans, but in the 1960s, it only came in liquid form in tin containers, like how we buy turpentine today. My job was to pour the Gunk into an old metal paint rolling pan, add five parts kerosene to one part Gunk, slide the pan under the motorcycle, then take an old stiff-bristle paint brush and scrub away any signs of leaking oil on the engine, which back in those days could be a significant amount of leakage for a Harley.

I actually considered it a fun chore and got great satisfaction out of turning an oily engine into a spotless assemblage of sand cast casings, polished aluminum covers, and bits of chrome accent. My favorite part always came after the job was complete. To this day, there is nothing that quite compares to the smell of a freshly-Gunked engine as it warms up to operating temperature. No, you wouldn't want to make it into a perfume, but, like the smell of leather or of the asphalt after it rains, it is an aroma that is strangely satisfying, and for me, full of fond memories.

Rolling north out of the Carolina's at a pace of 75 to 85 mph, the Harley's five-gallon fuel tank would hit reserve at around the 170-mile mark, necessitating a break to top the tank and obtain another time-stamped receipt. My first stop came just after sunup, or to be more precise, after the black of night was replaced by a dark gray that signaled day. I looked to the sky and donned my rain suit over the top of my leathers. Despite the previous day's assurances from my weather app, the sun itself would never actually make an appearance

on this trip, and "partly cloudy" manifested itself as "perpetual rain" starting at 9:00 a.m. The precipitation accompanied me all the way to Louisville and back again to Charlotte.

Occasionally, the rain fell in a light mist, but for much of the ride, it cascaded in blinding downpours that forced a significantly slower pace. Though my rain suit and full helmet were effective at keeping me dry, the temperatures dropped as the day wore on. By three in the afternoon, I reached Louisville and had to search out a Harley dealer to obtain winter weather gloves and additional insulation for my torso.

Back into the rain I charged, retracing my tire tracks toward Charlotte. At 11:00 p.m., and with a few hundred miles still to go, I began to feel sleepy. I pulled into a truck stop, downed a hot chocolate, and took a 45-minute catnap. Feeling refreshed, I attacked the highway once again and arrived back home at 2:30 Sunday morning. I slept soundly until around noon.

Assessment:

- 1000-mile days are extremely hard to do in conditions that hinder your average speed. This time it was weather, but on the "big ride" it could be traffic congestion, road construction, mechanical breakdowns, or simply the lack of freeways with elevated speed limits. Even in ideal conditions, a 1000-mile day eats up hours that extend into sleep time, either on the front end or the back end. It would be very imprudent to attempt two such days in a row. On our 48-state tour, we will need to space these days appropriately.

- The Harley performed flawlessly, never missing a beat, even when drenched. However, my 26-year-old motorcycle lacked a number of modern features I would have welcomed: GPS for guidance; Bluetooth for communication and entertainment; anti-lock brakes and traction control for better assurance of remaining upright; heated hand grips and seat for fighting the cold. Big Red is my baby, but I knew that I should leave her in the barn for the big trip, and I needed to shop for a bike with the desired upgrades.

- My body hits a big wall after 18 hours of riding. Even with my catnap, I had to scream out songs to myself to maintain alertness in the final few hours of the ride. This was foolish, and I later regretted pushing on, endangering both myself and others for the sake of my goal. If I could not find the discipline to ignore pressures to achieve the goal and to stop riding when seriously dangerous conditions arise, whether from within or without, I should not undertake the 48 State Challenge.

As my pilot brother, Monte, is fond of observing; *"Exceptional pilots use exceptional judgment to avoid exceptional circumstances that require exceptional skill."* In the coming year leading up to the big ride, Trent and I would have many serious discussions on this topic, making promises to one another to let the other person know if either of us feels a need for rest or to completely shut things down. The primary goal was to return home alive. The secondary goal was to complete the 48-state circuit, however long it takes. The last goal was to complete the circuit within 240 hours. We committed ourselves to these ordered priorities.

I submitted the map of my Louisville ride, my witness statements, and the gas receipts to the Iron Butt Association. A few weeks later, I received a package containing my certificate of accomplishment, including patches, stickers, and a license plate frame declaring I was now a full-fledged member of the Iron Butt Association and one of "The World's Toughest Riders." Recalling those last few hours of my ride, I thought that my emblems should read, "World's Toughest (and sometimes most foolish) Riders."

CHAPTER 5
RIDING FOR A CAUSE

In the summer of 2016, I was heavily involved with a charity cause focused on injured military veterans. I was vice president of operations for a major tire and automotive service franchise, and we had gotten behind The Independence Fund, an organization that is particularly known for providing tank-tracked, all-terrain motorized wheelchairs to veterans who had lost the use of their legs. It had been my privilege to present wheelchairs to veterans on the field at games for the Texas Rangers and Cleveland Indians baseball teams and Major League Soccer's Salt Lake Real. I asked the administrators of The Independence Fund if I could create a fundraiser through my 48-state Challenge. My thought was to obtain pledges, similar to a walk-a-thon, with folks pledging $1 per state that we pass through and doubling that amount if we completed the circuit within the ten days. The people at the Independence Fund were thrilled by the originality of the idea and supported my proposal.

Trent and I continued to plan our route. Because he was more limited on vacation days available than was I, we decided to start and end the ride in the West, which meant that prior to the start of the ride, I needed to get my bike from Charlotte to his home in Las Vegas. I could ship the motorcycle, but that would be expensive and risked damaging the bike. I could ride the motorcycle to Nevada, but that would add days to my trip and additional saddle fatigue to my backside. Eventually, this problem was solved when Mitch and his wife, Anne, offered to burn their measly one-weeks' vacation by flying themselves and their two little boys from their home near Salt Lake City to my home in Charlotte two weeks before the start of our big ride. They would then leave the boys with us while they rode my bike back to their home in Utah. This would provide them a wonderful motorcycle trip as a couple, allow my wife and I to spend time with our precious grandsons, and of course, it would place my motorcycle relatively close to our intended starting point for the big ride–a big win for everybody. Two days before the start of the big ride, I would simply fly to Salt Lake with my two grandsons in tow, retrieve my motorcycle, and ride it to Vegas to rendezvous with Trent. But what motorcycle would that be?

Both Trent and I needed to pick up new motorcycles for the ride. In the Fall of 2016, I began my search in earnest. Although the Harley Davidson brand has always appealed to me, and I've owned quite a few of them, I am no "motorcycle bigot," and I know there are many outstanding bikes out there from all makes. I have owned most brands. My search for the right motorcycle for this trip would be based purely on utility.

I had owned three BMW motorcycles up to this point, and I held a healthy respect for their functionality and reliability. Many of the most devoted and accomplished distance riders in the world choose BMWs as their mount, and after much investigation and a few test-rides, I purchased a BMW K1600GLT in November of 2016. Not only did the bike have all the modern features and accessories I desired, but it also happened to be the most powerful touring motorcycle on the planet, producing 160 horsepower, an incredible amount for a motorcycle. This bike put the "fun" into the word "function."

I added only two aftermarket items to this fully-loaded touring motorcycle: a luggage rack mounted to the top of the standard rear box (or trunk)–this would provide a place to strap on extra gear; I installed a set of rear crash bars designed to protect the beautiful and expensive fairing and saddlebags should the bike tip over. Weighing in at 768 lb. (before adding the rider and his gear), this Beemer was even more hefty than my fully-dressed Harley. And to make things even trickier in slow-speed maneuvers, the bike sat taller than the Harley, and the center of gravity made tip-overs a real possibility.

I took advantage of living in the warm South by getting in as many evening and weekend check-rides as I could during November and early December, and I became convinced that this motorcycle represented the epitome of two-wheel engineering.

As 2016 came to an end, Trent and I had finalized our route plan. As mentioned, the rules for the ride only required that we enter each of the lower 48 states, even if that was simply to get gas at a border town. We determined that the best starting point for day one of the trip would be the Southern Nevada town of Laughlin, situated across the Colorado River from Bullhead City, Arizona and just a few miles upstream from Needles, California. Within the first thirty minutes of riding, we could then capture three states and head east, focusing on *pinch points* where a number of state borders could be crossed in short order.

We found our pinch points in such places as the panhandle regions of Texas and Oklahoma where we would have the opportunity to move quickly from New Mexico to Texas, north to Oklahoma and Colorado, and east to Kansas, all within a few hours. Riding south along the Mississippi River from Missouri would allow us to catch Kentucky, Tennessee, Arkansas, Mississippi, and Louisiana simply by crossing back and forth across the river. With an eye focused on maximizing "states touched" while minimizing miles covered, we plotted the course and usually found that interstate highways were the best choice, though state routes or county roads occasionally became our best or only options. Our final solution would cover 8,136 miles with the final leg hooking through the Northwest states and dropping us down into the topside of Utah, our 48th state.

We had also decided to start the trip on May 27th, the Saturday of Memorial Day weekend. Not only would this be appropriate given the veterans' cause we were promoting, but it also provided Trent with an extra holiday to augment his limited allotment of vacation time.

About this time, Trent created a Facebook page he named "Stephenson 48 State Charity Ride" so that our friends could follow our preparations and track our progress on the ride. As the name suggests, we had associated ourselves with The Independence Fund in support of veterans, and Trent set up a Go Fund Me link with a goal to raise $2,000 for our wounded military heroes. We soon found ourselves with a couple hundred followers from around the world, and we kept them updated on developments as we entered 2017 and continued our preparations for the trip.

As awareness for our ride grew, so did inquiries from friends around the country who either invited us to drop by to say hello as we traveled through or (for those who rode motorcycles themselves) asked if they could join us for a segment of the ride near their locality. Few seemed to grasp that this would be a race against the clock where breaks would be minimized and choreographed like a NASCAR pitstop. Every extra minute sitting still would represent one and a third miles lost.

We also didn't know exactly when we would be passing through any given point on the course. Sure, we had daily goals, but these were subject to alteration for any number of reasons, and we knew that on any given day, we would be either a few hundred miles ahead of schedule or just as many miles behind. We tried to be cool about it, and we sincerely appreciated their friendly outreach, but we had to decline arranging rendezvous with our supporters along the way.

The only exceptions were those who expressed interest in riding out with us from Laughlin on the first day who would then turn around at an appropriate point to return home. My brother-in-law, Steve, bought his BMW K1200 just to be a part of the start of our charge across the continent, and another good friend, Don Turley, expressed his intentions to ride his Ducati with us on the eve of our journey as we rode from Las Vegas to Laughlin.

As spring approached, our plans came together, and the primary missing component was a motorcycle for Trent. He was just moving to new digs in Las Vegas and was somewhat limited on funds, so the budget called for a modestly-priced used motorcycle. He wanted to go with an adventure touring motorcycle (think "giant dirt bike" with saddlebags and a windshield), but most of the bikes in his price range were quite old and fairly worn. He finally found a 2006 Buell Odyssey 1200 with low miles and in sound condition. The Buell Motor Company was an off-shoot, of sorts, from Harley Davidson and utilized Harley engines to create higher performance motorcycles. The company ceased operations in 2009, so used Buells could be had for a relatively low investment. This seemed like a good way to obtain a capable bike within Trent's price range. We figured that the 1200 Sportster engine was well-proven, and it was one we were both familiar with, having owned Sportsters ourselves. The only parts we were unfamiliar with were the peripheral add-ons and special computer engine mapping that enhanced the performance. That lack of familiarity would prove to be detrimental to us in times to come.

Trent purchased the Buell in Utah and rode it back to Las Vegas. Unfortunately, the ride home revealed a computer glitch that caused the motor to partially shut down from elevated engine temperatures that occur when riding above 80 mph. Trent and I both knew that this would not be acceptable for our brisk jaunt across America, and he sought solutions at motorcycle shops and on internet forums, but the answer remained elusive as the month of May loomed closer. Every few days, I checked in with Trent to see if the issue was resolved.

On April 28th, exactly one month from the start of our big ride, I received word that one of my business associates had been struck and killed as he rode his Harley toward a motorcycle gathering in Laughlin, Nevada, (by chance, the same location we had selected for the start of our journey). The description of the accident made it clear that there was nothing the rider could have done to avoid the impaired driver who crossed the centerline on a curve. It was a simple case of "wrong place at the wrong time," and it served as a very sobering reminder that this is a dangerous sport and that even proper preparation and well-honed skills cannot save a motorcyclist from the wholly unpredictable.

We were two weeks away from our planned start when Mitch and Anne flew to Charlotte with their two boys. The BMW was far more sophisticated than anything Mitch had ridden, and we spent a day familiarizing him with such things as the computer "mouse" device on the left hand grip and all the available features/functions. I had purchased two helmet-to-helmet radios with Bluetooth cell phone capability to be used by Trent and me on our trip. Mitch and Anne would test these out on their three-day ride back to Utah.

One anticipated problem that could really slow down our lap around America is the matter of tire wear, particularly on the BMW. To get the desired traction, motorcycle tires are much softer in composition than automobile tires, and the rear tires on my model of BMW are known to wear out in five or six thousand miles while the front tires may last twice that distance. Trent's Buell had new rubber front and rear and was known to be much easier on tire wear than my heavier and more powerful Beemer. His Buell could complete the trip on one set, but my Beemer...

When I purchased the BMW in Charlotte, I told the dealership about my intended ride, and they offered to support me in any way they could. I knew that even if Mitch and Anne headed to Utah on new tires, the rear tire would surely be worn out by the time I swung back through North Carolina on my 48-state challenge. I asked the dealership to be prepared to offer me lightning-fast "pit stop" service when I rode through on day four of my ride. I needed the proper tires on-hand and mechanics standing by to turn the bike around as quickly as possible, which on motorcycles, still requires a few hours. The BMW service manager assured me they would be ready for me when I arrived.

Mitch and Anne's ride to Utah went smoothly. They took in the notoriously twisty road known as "Tail of the Dragon" near The Great Smoky Mountains national park and followed the route of the Trail of Tears as they rode into the Cherokee Nation in Oklahoma. There they stopped to check on our family's tribal registration status, (we are proud of our Cherokee heritage), and then they crossed the Rockies on I-70 to reach Utah safe and sound. Mitch reported that the BMW functioned flawlessly, and he promised to have it cleaned up and ready to go when I arrived on the 25th.

As the day of my departure from Charlotte neared, my wife became a bit more nervous about the ride. She was well aware that fluke-but-fatal mishaps are far too common on motorcycles. She knew that even "simple" motor vehicle mishaps can become serious issues for a motorcyclist. Getting rear-ended at a stop light can give a car driver whiplash, but when this happens to an unprotected biker, his spine may be snapped on the grill of the incoming car. Collisions with deer and other wildlife typically result in dented fenders for car drivers, while motorcyclists don't fare these encounters nearly so well. And dropping a wheel off onto the shoulder in a moment of inattention is not a catastrophe for calm-headed car drivers, but it can be quite the rodeo when one is on a bike.

Donna bought a tracking device designed to use satellite technology to search for such things as lost keys. Attached to my motorcycle, it would allow her to keep tabs on where we were at any given time. Tracking us on her home computer, she would be able to see if we were moving along on the map on her screen, and if so, she would know we were still safe and sound.

CHAPTER 6
THE DAYS PRECEDING THE LAUNCH

Wednesday, May 24th arrived—the day of my departure from Charlotte. The four-hour flight to Salt Lake City was never to be forgotten, and hopefully never to be repeated. My normally well-behaved grandsons, Logan and Ayden, ages three and 18 months, were more than a handful once we took to the skies. My wife had prepped me with bags of toys, snacks, books, and an iPad loaded with kiddie games, but one hour into the flight, the toddler insisted on roaming the plane, and the three-year-old got ill. I might have been able to handle one of these boys alone, but I couldn't take care of one without the other one resorting to tears.

By nature, I'm sensitive to the feelings of others, and I hate to be a burden or imposition on anyone, so I was red-faced but grateful for the resourceful flight attendants and for an angelic woman in the seat in front of me who proved to be a very capable grandmother herself. The boys went to sleep just in time for us to land in Salt Lake City, and I was certain that nothing I would face on the road during the coming weeks would be half as challenging as what I had just endured.

At my son's home outside of Salt Lake City, I combined the gear I had sent ahead with Mitch with the items I had brought with me from Charlotte and loaded the bike. There were five loading zones:

- A tank bag strapped onto the fuel tank in front of me became the ideal place for items I may wish to access while on the road

- A large rear box with a hinged lid would be the go-to storage space for items we needed quick access to during our fuel stops
- Two hard-shell saddlebags attached on each side of the rear wheel. One of these was fully devoted to clothing and toiletries, and the other to bad weather gear, a tool kit, and items to care for the bike.
- The rear (passenger) seat was ideal for strapping a weatherproof duffel containing sleeping bags (this also served as a comfy backrest for the rider).
- The luggage rack atop the rear box served as the strapping platform for our tent and, as we shed layers on hot days, a place to strap chaps or heavy jackets.

Motorcyclists get very particular about their personal riding gear. For one, good protection is expensive and modern riding apparel features sewn-in armor to help protect key areas in an accident. Riding gear also tends to be chosen based on the personality of the rider and the type of riding he or she identifies with. I've never gone for the "Hell's Angels" look, nor have I gone in for the "spaceman" styles of many adventure riders. My pants are reinforced denim covered, generally, with a set of leather chaps. My jacket is a heavy brown leather with internal armor – no patches proclaiming anything and no blingy silver buckles, zippers, or snaps. I've had this jacket for twenty years and it is my second-favorite jacket of all time.

THE SCAB

Sometime in the 1950s, Mom and Dad bought matching gray leather Harley Davidson jackets.

Dad wearing his jacket on their 1960 trip from Kansas City to Salt Lake City

By this time, these jackets would have shown scuff marks from where Mom and Dad slid out in Old Mexico, the blemishes providing their late-arriving friend, Bob Hunt, the only clue that they'd been down. Over the next decade and a half, the jackets became a little road-worn from weathering the rains, the summer sun, and perhaps another spill or two.

Mom wearing her jacket from that very ride.

In 1974, at age sixteen, I commandeered Dad's jacket for our 7,000-mile ride across the US, and from that time on, the old gray jacket became mine. By then, the original sheen of the leather had worn away, and there were portions on the shoulders and elbows that looked like gray suede where road rash had attempted to wear through. Other portions showed fine and superficial cracks that checkered themselves across the various panels. The jacket was so stiff that, even when taken off, the arms kept their barrel shape. For me, a six-foot-tall, 130-pound teenager self-conscious about his spindly body, this jacket was like slipping on artificial muscles. Suddenly, I looked *built*– my shoulders were broader, and my stringy arms took on a bulky definition. I took to snapping only the bottom button because I thought it gave my torso a V shape as though I'd spent months in the gym. I wore the jacket as I rode to high school and then kept it on throughout the day even in the sweltering Florida heat. It was miserable, but vanity has its price, and I was willing to pay. The photos below are from that 1974 ride.

On that ride, I went down a few times myself–never at high speed–and each time the jacket gathered a few more scars and scuffs. Dad took to calling the jacket "The Scab," and I continued to wear The Scab well into my twenties before this relic was forced into retirement. So– what happened to The Scab?

In 1981, our family (Mom, Dad, my siblings, and their wives) held a reunion at Panguitch Lake in Southern Utah. Donna and I drove up from Las Vegas in my truck, taking our camping gear and following a veritable caravan of Stephenson vehicles to the lake. My younger brother, Monte, had to work late on the day we all headed out, and I told him he could ride my 1980 Harley Electra Glide to join us.

After work, Monte headed north out of Vegas on my Hog in the company of a family friend, Tracy, who was riding a Honda. About ten o'clock that night, on a dark stretch of Hwy 89, a deer tried to dart across the road just as an 18-wheeler came over a rise in time to knock that deer down, dead as a tree stump. Right behind that semi-truck were two motorcycle riders– Monte and Tracy. They came over that rise, and as their headlight beams dropped to reveal the asphalt in front of them, they saw the deer's body lying across the road, but it was too late. They both hit the carcass, and both bikes were airborne at 70 mph. They landed hard on their wheels, wobbled once or twice, then the bikes went down.

Following right behind the motorcycles was a car carrying a young family. When they came over the rise in the road, they saw motorcycles sliding headlight/taillight down the road in front of them, both leaving rooster-tails of sparks. When the car bounded over the deer carcass, the driver was sure he'd just ran over a motorcyclist. Fortunately, the boys had slid off the road in time to be missed by the automobile. The deer, after having been run over by twenty-six tires on four vehicles, represented some very well-tenderized venison.

It was midnight when a sheriff's deputy drove into the Stephenson camp at Panguitch Lake and informed us of the accident. He assured Mom and Dad that the boys were fine, but that they had some pretty bad road rash and were in the local hospital. Of secondary importance, but still of interest to me, I learned that my Harley was in the local tow-yard.

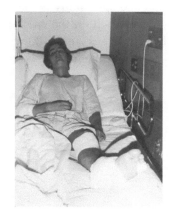

The boys healed up within a couple of months, and the black Harley was brought back to life in a gorgeous two-toned black and silver. Unfortunately, the only permanent casualty (besides the deer) was a thirty-year-old faded gray motorcycle jacket that offered its last full measure of devotion by helping to protect my little brother as he skidded along a darkened Utah highway.

The right sleeve is shredded, and a few ripped seams exposed the inner lining. It's clearly no longer road-worthy, but somehow, I've never been able to toss it away. To this day, The Scab hangs in an honored spot in my home–a faded American flag, folded into a triangle, rests within the crook of its left sleeve. A shrine? No–not really. But if there is such a thing as the "fabric of motorcycling," one of its emblems, tattered and worn, hangs on my wall.

On Thursday morning, May 25th, I headed south from Tooele on Hwy 36, an often-desolate two-laner stretching through ranch and mining country. I continued south to the town of Delta where I caught US 50 east to I-15, and I was able to put the hammer down for Vegas. The day's ride would cover "just" 420 miles, but that is only half of what we would need to cover each day beginning on Saturday.

After many decades of distance-riding, many highways have become familiar to me, and I often encountered memories laying right in the middle of the road–ghosts and shadows that reignite smiles, tears, and sometimes winces. Some of those memories warm the heart; some are melancholy as thoughts turn to those no longer riding with me. Others elicit a simple shake of the head. As I-15 gradually descends from the Wasatch range of the Rockies to the deserts of Nevada, the road runs south through a series of great steps as passes connect one valley to another in a series of changes of elevation that reminded me of locks on the Panama Canal. A little north of Cove Fort, I descended an incline I remembered well.

In the spring of 1980, I was a student at Brigham Young University in Provo, Utah, and had spent my spring break visiting my folks in Las

Vegas. In those days, before the internet and before weather apps were available to warn of troubles ahead, I'd check the weather section of the newspaper, look up at the skies before mounting my bike, then head out if things looked good. On the Saturday morning that concluded my visit with the folks, the skies were clear, so I rolled north. My transport that day was a Honda 750 Four.

Three hours later, I hit Cedar City, Utah, in a blizzard complete with whiteout conditions, and by the time I passed through Beaver, most cars had exited the highway. A few truckers continued to accompany me on the slab of snow that fully obscured the pavement–only the reflector markers protruding from the drifts on the left and on the right provided clues to where the highway lies.

I rode through chilling valleys, but they were not a particular problem as far as the grade of the road was concerned. It was when I came to those aforementioned mountain passes that my bike slowed as the rear tire spun in a desperate search for traction on the steep inclines, and I lowered both boots to "ski the ground" to remain upright. The spokes of my wheels were packed solid with ice, and my mount became more ice sickle than *motorsickle*.

In North of Cove Fort, I ascended a pass that sent me spinning and sprawling across the empty lanes more than once. I struggled to find solid enough footing to leverage the motorcycle back to its wheels while I kept an eye out for any eighteen-wheelers emerging from the veil of white behind me. Too broke to afford a motel and too young to realize the danger, I continued onward to my destination, arriving twelve hours after beginning my journey.

———

Thirty-seven years after that chilling adventure, I rode south through that same pass, glancing over at those northbound lanes where my Honda and I had wallowed in the snow, and I shivered again in the warm May breeze.

As I arrived in Las Vegas, I stopped by my brother-in-law's house. Steve had purchased a used BMW R/S, and he was focused on earning his 1000-miles-in-one-day certificate from the Iron Butt Association. His intention was to ride with us for our first 500 miles, then turn around and ride back to Nevada that same day. He was not an experienced long-distance rider (primarily a dirt bike rider), and he wanted me to check out his bike.

The RS, with its compact fairing/windscreen, short clip-on bars, and forward riding position, is more of a sport bike than a long-distance touring motorcycle. Steve asked me to take it for a spin and to give him my opinion regarding its suitability for a 1000-mile day. It didn't take me long to reach a verdict.

One of the keys to fighting fatigue on long rides is having the ability to shift riding positions from time to time rather than being locked into one single stance. In my opinion, the best long-distance machines have the foot controls mounted in the center of the bike so that the pegs or footboards carry at least some of the rider's weight (I loathe forward-mounted controls for distance-riding). Centered pegs/footboards will allow a rider to stand while riding to relieve a cramp or to ease the impact of a large bump or divot, while maintaining easy access to the controls. Additionally, auxiliary highway pegs mounted forward on the bike afford options for temporarily stretching out the legs and the rear passenger pegs may serve as yet another option. As the rider moves his or her feet to these various peg options, the butt-to-saddle *contact patch* varies enough to provide relief to crotch and glutes. For a while, it's "right foot forward" on the highway pegs and "left foot back" on the passenger pegs. A little bit later, a rider can reverse this position and can feel a significant difference, almost as if he or she had changed to a different seat. Unfortunately, Steve's RS only offered one placement for the feet, although the pegs were, at least, well centered.

The stubby handlebars sported by the RS only allowed one position for the upper torso. The rider has no choice but to lean forward over the tank with his head cocked back to see the road ahead. The short windshield did little to knock away the persistent 85 mph winds to the face or, worse yet, the raindrops-turned-bullets that sting at high speeds. On this motorcycle, the ergonomics were resolute and unforgiving, and a 1000-mile ride would require a greater measure of determination and endurance than I deemed necessary or sensible. I reported my concerns to Steve, but he remained undaunted.

We gave his bike a thorough *pre-flight* inspection: fluids checked, air pressure set, bolts wrenched. The gear was checked; it must be made fast so that it won't come loose even after hours of hanging on in gale-force winds and despite the incessant buzz from engine vibrations. It was a ritual I'd learned forty years earlier.

———

In 1974, my dad and I and my two younger brothers headed out on the aforementioned 7000-mile circuit of America. I was sixteen, my brother Scott was fourteen, and Monte was just eleven.

By day nine of the ride, we had already traversed the southern portion of the country from Florida to the Grand Canyon and had rolled north along the Rockies to Yellowstone before turning east to cross the plains to the Black Hills of South Dakota. In the course of those nine days, I had become weary of my dad's frequently offered advice on riding techniques and road safety. I'd been riding motorcycles since the age of eight and had never been in a serious accident. I saw myself as both a skilled and conscientious rider, and I began to resent Dad's inference that I was a novice in need of his repeated reminders, warnings, and observations.

We had pitched our tents one night in a campground high in the Black Hills National Forest and arose a little after sunrise to start our day.

These pictures were taken by Dad at that very campsite as we boys downed the Pop Tarts and the canned peaches that were our typical breakfast (easy to store in saddlebags). I wrote daily in a journal I still have today.

We broke camp and loaded our gear onto the motorcycles, and by this point in the trip, the loading of the bikes involved a specific order for every sleeping bag, tent, and backpack, each situated in a pre-designated location. Scott and I loaded the Beemer, then I fired it up and we both climbed aboard, ready for the day. Dad finished fastening gear onto the Honda before walking over to double-check our load. Turning my head away, I pursed my lips and rolled my eyes in resentment as Dad tugged on the bungees and shook the pack to make sure we had done our job correctly. He then asked me if I'd pulled the dipstick yet.

"Yes!" I hissed with teenage attitude that caused Dad to raise an eye toward me. My tone softened only slightly as I continued, "The oil is halfway up the stick." Dad nodded then motioned me over to his motorcycle where he unfolded a map over his fuel tank and gave me a quick overview of our route for the morning.

So far on the trip, Dad almost always took lead as we rode, with me following behind, but on this morning, I felt like exerting some independence, perhaps even some defiance. I rolled out of camp ahead of Dad. We were soon on the narrow two-lane road that descended the hills toward the plains.

The descent called for a series of switchbacks running serpentine down the heavily forested slope, and each hairpin turn required a downshift into second or even first gear for the negotiation of the curve. Such curves are great fun for motorcyclists as the bike is brought into the turn *wide* (to the outside of the arc) and then stuffed in tight to be close to the centerline at the turn's apex. Then, with a little throttle applied, the bike exits the curve moving back out *wide* again.

I entered the first few curves with some apprehension, then became more comfortable with each successive turn. After nine or ten curves, I noticed that, on the straightaways, I could peer downhill through the trees to catch glimpses of the road rising to meet me at the next hairpin. I realized that by looking through the trees I could determine whether or not traffic was coming up the road to greet me at the curve. When there was no oncoming car, I could dive deeper into the hairpin, crossing the centerline to make use of both lanes for a more rapid ride through the turn. Yes, Dad had previously warned me against doing this, but given that I could see any traffic on the rising road, I was unconcerned and continued my brisk pace.

Approaching a tight left-hand hairpin, I checked through the trees and saw no vehicles on the road below. I applied minimal brake before entering wide and dove in tight. I crossed the centerline into the oncoming lane when I heard a squeal of tires, and I read the word "Plymouth" stretching across the widest chrome grill I'd ever seen. My brother's knees squeezed tight on my hips as I thrusted the handlebars to dive the bike to the right to avoid the seemingly unavoidable collision. In less than a second, I became simultaneously aware that we had avoided contact with the Plymouth and that we immediately had a new problem. We were now pointed perpendicular to our intended direction of travel, and within a few more feet, we would launch off the edge of the road and tumble down the mountainside. Another desperate wrangling of the bars rolled the bike hard left as the tires bit tight to the asphalt at the edge of the road before we skidded on the pea gravel, drifting wide onto the scant twenty-four inches of available shoulder. The pebbles flew, the Beemer danced, but we remained upright, and I was able to bring it back onto the pavement. Astonished, we found ourselves again rolling unharmed down the road.

My heart pounded as my breath caught. I kept the throttle at idle and the motorcycle slowed despite the descending grade. A glance in my mirrors showed Dad rapidly approaching, and I expected he would angrily instruct me to pull over. To my surprise, Dad rode right past without so much as a nod of the head. I gingerly applied throttle to fall in behind.

Had Dad missed seeing what I had done? No—he had been riding right behind me, and his attention would have been fully centered on the upcoming turn. Besides, Dad doesn't miss much. Surely the screeching of the brakes and subsequent sounding of the car horn had registered a loud protest of my foolishness that no one could miss. Scott shouted into my helmet a flat declaration of what I already knew, "Dad's going to kill you."

Despite the many times during my childhood and youth that I was certain my dad was "going to kill me," he never once actually put my mortality on the line, though I did grow up in a time when corporal punishment was used to great effect. While I knew a whoopin' at my age was quite unlikely, I dreaded the in-my-face, drill-sergeant-like tongue-lashing I knew was coming my way. It was going to be brutal.

We rode for another hour and a half before Dad gave me the signal that his fuel tank had just hit reserve, so we needed to pull in at the next filling station. My heart rate rose again as I knew the time had come for me to face the consequences of my actions.

We found a station and pulled in, bringing both bikes up to the same pump as we always did. We shut the motors down and my brothers both climbed off and disappeared into the station, ostensibly to use the restroom, but more likely, to avoid the specter of Dad's wrath descending upon me. As all siblings know, fallout from parental ire is a very real thing, and you don't want to risk being included in the collateral damage.

Dad filled his tank first then handed the nozzle to me. As I filled my tank, Dad reached into a saddlebag and retrieved the map. I fueled the Beemer then hung the nozzle onto the pump as Dad approached.

He laid the map on top of my tank and pointed out the route ahead, telling me what highway numbers to watch for. No anger. No disappointment. No sign that he was even thinking about the near tragedy that still fully occupied my own mind. Dad paid for the gas, my brothers climbed back aboard, and we resumed the ride.

Throughout the day, at every gas stop, when we paused for lunch, when we pulled over to take in a scenic view, I expected the lecture that didn't come, and I became concerned that perhaps Dad was only building up his anger. Finally, that evening after we had heated some Dinty Moore stew over the campfire, a time of silence settled in, and we all just stared into the fire. I couldn't take the tension any longer.

"Dad–this morning–when I nearly parted the grill of that Plymouth," I breathed deep, not knowing really what to ask, but I continued, "You haven't said anything."

Dad's gaze remained on the fire for a long moment before speaking up softly, still not looking in my direction. "Son, I've seen a lot in my years of riding–I've experienced an awful lot, and some of it has been very painful. I have center-punched cars– I've center-punched cows– I've hit, and I've been hit in ways that were surprising to me at the time. For every injury I've sustained, I've witnessed a dozen serious or fatal incidents involving friends or associates, and I've experienced a hundred near misses of my own. All of these things feed into how I ride, and they make me a better rider."

He looked at me, "More than anything, Wes, I wish I could transfer those experiences from my head to yours so that you could have all the advantages that experience can offer, and you *could* have it if only you really and truly believed those things that I share with you and the advice I offer you."

He paused for a moment, then sighed and continued, "How many cars will you have to hit, or be hit by, before you will trust in the counsel of those who have been down the road before you? Will it take a broken body? Will you ever manage to buy into the experience of others before your skepticism and arrogance kills you?"

He looked back to the fire and shook his head, "I don't know how to make you believe me, son. It's your choice. It's all up to you."

I spent a long night staring up at the ceiling of my tent. I thought about this concept of "transferring experience" from the one who originally went through the pains of gaining those insights to the person, perhaps new to the scene, who has a real need for understanding and for an awareness of the costly lessons learned. I did not want to be doomed to rediscover painful truths. I could see that by reaching out with an open mind for knowledge possessed by predecessors I would be on the preferred path to become wise beyond my years, and I felt a new hunger to gather intel on the roads in front of me, not just as a motorcycle rider, but in broader aspects of life as I could sense that my father's words held implications far beyond road safety.

We broke camp the next morning and loaded the gear onto the motorcycles as the sun rose on another glorious day. I was the first to get my packs cinched down tight, and I fired up the Beemer to let Dad know I was ready to roll.

Well, *almost* ready. I sat there idling, pleased to wait until Dad could come over to double-check my load.

In Vegas, after giving Steve's bike a good look-over, I rode to my daughter's home where I would stay the night.

Daughter Kimberly and her husband Corey are the parents of our then four-year-old twin granddaughters Chloe and Brooke. These active and chatty little sprites provided an early highlight to my adventure as a visit with them brings a satisfaction that only another grandparent can understand. Trent joined us for dinner that evening, and he rode over on the Buell, my first opportunity to lay eyes on the machine, and I was able to take it for a spin.

I was pleased to find that the Buell sat well (certainly compared to Steve's RS) with a fairly upright seating position and with the pegs situated in the center of the bike. The saddle was comfortable and provided opportunity for shifting positions. The saddlebags were spacious, and the rear luggage rack could lay flat for strapping on large items or articulate to perpendicular to serve as a backrest and support for a backpack. The windshield was quite small, but Trent claimed that he would rely on his full-face helmet and weather gear when things turned nasty, and I knew that many riders of adventure tour bikes did just fine on long rides with minimal protective bodywork on their bikes. The Buell appeared to be in good condition and pulled strong and smooth. I asked if Trent felt he had repaired the computer problem with the engine, and he wasn't certain that this was resolved, having not yet had the opportunity to test repairs at high speeds for a long distance. However, a knowledgeable technician had recommended an aftermarket part that he claimed was a sure fix for this issue, and the part was being overnighted to Trent's house. We would need to install this on Friday before we headed to Laughlin. I was quite frustrated that we still had this issue to deal with, an issue that had the potential of jeopardizing our entire trip.

Trent and I ate dinner with Kim and her family, after which he and I reviewed the maps one more time. Or, more accurately, I reviewed the maps while Trent sat next to me with his attention split between the riding plan and the never-ending texts from his friends. His attitude seemed to be, "How complex can this be? We zig-zag east until we hit the Atlantic then turn north."

In addition to the course strategy, we reviewed our logistic plans for our fuel stops, and I reminded Trent about a few points of safety, particularly the point I have always stressed to my kids who ride, "You gotta always be on the hunt for your killer." My kids knew what I meant. We needed to ride with an eye out for the car or truck driver that would take your life if you let them. This idea harks back to lessons I learned from the harshest ride-master I've ever known: my own father.

———

During high school, my older brother, Jeff, had a best friend whom everybody called "Duck" for reasons I never was able to discover. From my perspective as a 12-year-old, Duck seemed to have it all: a pretty girlfriend, popularity, a car, and a beautiful Yamaha SX650 motorcycle. He and Jeff were riding buddies, and I idolized them both. Like other teenagers in the neighborhood, Duck loved spending time with my dad, talking motorcycles, wrenching on motorcycles, and riding motorcycles.

One day, a phone call came informing us that Duck had been in a serious motorcycle accident. Jeff and Dad headed to the hospital to provide what support they could to the family. Upon their return, I rushed to meet them, and I learned that Duck was not in mortal danger, but he would be in a body cast during many months of recovery. Jeff told me that the accident occurred at an Y intersection on Old Dixie Highway, and I knew the location well. Duck had the right-away, but a woman in a car turned left and hit our friend nearly head-on. She was cited by the police for failure to yield.

My dad stood across the living room as Jeff related the story, and at the conclusion of Jeff's account, Dad approached my brother and me and flat out stated, "This was Duck's fault. He should have expected this."

Jeff and I were stunned by the harshness of Dad's declaration. Our friend was in a hospital bed with rods inserted into his legs because an inattentive driver disregarded her responsibility to yield to oncoming traffic. But Dad was resolute as he continued, "You'll never see a head-stone carved with, 'But at least it wasn't his fault.' There's just no solace in that. No motorcyclist can lean on 'what ought to happen' out on the road. You have to look for it; you have to expect it; you must make the other driver prove that they are not going to kill you. It's no fun; it slows you down; it means you can never relax–that you can never assume the best. You have to ride on edge."

We knew Dad was angry. He was angry at the driver of the car. He apparently had some anger for Duck. But mostly, he was angry at himself for not better preparing the young rider, and he knew that it could just as well have been one of his own boys approaching the same intersection with the same situation. He could sense– no, he *knew*, that we rode with a dangerous innocence that he wanted to drive out of us in our approach to riding motorcycles.

His harsh words have had a lifelong effect on me. For many years, I've had a fear that, if I were to die on a motorcycle, regardless of the reason, my dad would look down into my casket, shake his head and mutter, "You stupid boy."

Nightmares aside, in a beneficial way, Dad made me feel that, not only was I responsible for what *I* was doing on the road, but that I was also responsible for what those around me on the road were doing. I had to ride as if I was an air traffic controller, watching out for all these other flight paths around me, each mindlessly going in their varied directions, with my primary purpose to make sure none of these would errantly cross my path.

––––––

Dad was right. It does take away from the fun. It causes your right wrist to shut down the speed a thousand times when it turns out that you didn't really need to, as it ended up just another one of countless false alarms. It means that you can never turn your head to take in a beautiful vista while there is an oncoming car about to blow past. Sure, the chances are slim that the car will cross the centerline while you are enjoying the view, but you can't afford to trust that. Some things are unforgiving and final, with no do-overs afforded.

This doesn't mean that you have to head for the ditch and hide at the approach of every car. It simply means that you must improve your odds by being ready on the brakes, watching for direct eye contact, avoiding blind spots, and looking for escape routes.

Of all the skill sets that can come into play in the world of motorcycling, this is perhaps the most important: the ability to never shift the responsibility for your life and for your safety to the traffic laws and to other people's obedience to the same. Like Dad said, there's just no solace in a tombstone reading, "But at least it wasn't his fault."

CHAPTER 7
THE EVE OF THE LAUNCH
FRIDAY, MAY 26TH

After an early morning shower, I ran a small load of laundry, then tightly rolled the clean clothes as I packed them and my toiletry kit into their assigned places in the saddle bags. The rest of the day, until late afternoon, was spent running errands with Kim and enjoying time at a park with my twin granddaughters. Despite keeping busy, my mind returned to the big ride as I searched my past experiences for a clue into what I might have overlooked or what I had forgotten to plan for. I was aware that this was a fool's errand. I had learned long ago that rides like this were all about the unexpected, the things you just can't plan for. Perhaps that's a good thing because the unexpected encounters can be the most memorable, as I learned on my very first road trip as commander of my own motorcycle.

———

In the summer of 1972, my dad was charged with negotiating contracts on behalf of Trans World Airlines with businesses scattered around the globe. He was often away for weeks at a time. Dad made every attempt to maximize what time he could with each of us kids. One of those efforts resulted in me, at just fourteen years of age, flying to Europe to spend a week with Dad in the beautiful country of Greece. It would be here that my inaugural road trip as the man behind the handlebars would take place.

Dad had arranged for a small hotel room off the beaten path in the

Athens neighborhood of Glyfada. After two days of seeing the local sites, we rented a pair of small-displacement Yamaha street bikes at a shop in downtown Athens. Dad mounted up and shouted over his shoulder, "Follow me!"

Apparently, Dad didn't realize that, despite my six years of dirt bike experience, I had never ridden in traffic of any kind–not on the roads of America and certainly nothing like the intense swarm he dove into on the ancient streets of Athens. Knowing that if I lost sight of Dad, I'd have no chance of finding him again, I dropped the motorcycle into gear and took off after him.

Though there were divider lines painted onto the pavement to define the lanes, there were no real positional rules in Athens. If there was any space at all for a car, scooter, bicycle, or motorcycle anywhere between the buildings to the right and the buildings to the left, that space was claimed in the teeming mass of metal that maneuvered and meshed as millions made their way through the Grecian capitol.

Dad joined in the mechanical melee like a native, sounding his horn and splitting the lanes as I drew in deep breaths and fought to keep up. With white knuckles I followed Dad as we skirted the base of the Acropolis. At the first stoplight, Dad maneuvered between cars to arrive at the front of the swarm. I followed with not more than an inch of clearance between my handlebar grips and the doors and fenders of the cars on either side. At the front of the pack, I glanced back at the horde of Citroen's, Fiats, Lancia's, and Alfa Romeos revving their engines. I wasn't sure our little two-stroke Yamahas could clear out of their way in time, and I remember thinking, "Easy on the clutch, boy– kill the motor here and it'll be like falling down in the running of the bulls."

South out of Athens, we took the coastal road that paralleled the beaches of the Saronic Gulf on our right. Occasional marinas held an eclectic mixture of watercraft, from teak inboard runabouts and sleek alabaster yachtery to old lateen-sailed sloops, (all colored dull blue with faded red trim), conjuring up mythological scenes of heroic journeys.

As I followed Dad through the curves, the echoes came of every story I'd ever heard Dad tell of two men, two motorcycles, and the open highway. Though the day's journey had just begun, I felt like I'd already arrived at a destination I'd dreamed about from my earliest memories.

We lunched near Cape Sounion then rode up to the ruins of the Temple of Poseidon, presiding high on a bluff overlooking the sea. Dad and I walked among the crumbled columns, and Dad's hand rested on my shoulder as we stood on the cliff, gazing out over the emerald waters.

According to legend, it was here that King Aegeus, founder of Athens, had stood looking out to sea, watching for the return of his son, Theseus, who had ventured forth intent on killing the mighty Minotaur. If Theseus prevailed against the beast, the returning ships were to hoist white sails, but if the prince had lost his life, black sails were to be flown from the masts. Tragically, the victorious Theseus forgot these instructions and his ships displayed the black sails as they approached the waiting King. In his distress at the perceived loss of his son, Aegeus cast himself from the cliff and met his end in the waters that would thereafter be known as the Aegean Sea.

Though the significance escaped me at the time, I've since recognized the appropriateness of this legendary tale of a father, of a son, of high adventure, and of deep bonds of love. The story, taken in at the start of what would become, for Dad and me, countless miles of joint discovery and enrichment, shared passions and enthrallment, and mutual appreciation for a world that passed through us even as we passed through its innumerable pinnacles, plains, and valleys.

We rode north from Cape Sounion, skirting the rocky eastern coast before turning inland at Thoricus. We kept within the 120 kph speed limits on these two-lane highways, and we did this for two reasons: first; we had to flog these little Yamahas just to maintain 100 kph (65 mph) so speeding wasn't a serious likelihood; second, and foremost, we wanted to avoid the police. I did not have a driver's license–I was not a legal driver even in the US, so we were sure that the Greek authorities would consider my papers to not be in order. We knew that legal troubles overseas could lead to prolonged jail time and hefty fines (a.k.a. payola).

I no longer recall the name of the little town, but I remember that it lay in a broad valley surrounded by low mountains of beige with slashes of white, assumedly scarred by quarrymen over the past few millennia. As we approached, well before we reached any of the buildings that would normally mark the town limits, we saw many vehicles parked along the side of the road. Men, women, and children carried baskets and toted folding chairs as they trod toward the town. Large colorful banners, all written in Greek, stretched high across the road between telephone poles. It appeared that the town was holding some sort of festival, and we were just in time to take it in.

As we entered the town, folks lining the streets waved enthusiastically, and we nodded back. As we rounded the first corner, we noticed large bales of hay lining the curbs, and around the next intersection, the bales formed a near-solid barrier across the road. True to European driving tradition (if your vehicle can fit through a space, poke it in there), dad slipped his motorcycle between two bales, and I followed.

As we passed the bales and continued onto the empty street beyond, the crowds on the sidewalk became quite animated, waving their arms at us like we had just liberated their country. It was then that we heard the growing din of high-revving engines echoing off the surrounding buildings. An instant later, Dad swerved his motorcycle to the right, aiming for the sidewalk, and his quick dive fully revealed the road before us was filled with Ferraris, Lotuses, and Porches– their headlights taped over and numbers on their hoods–screaming straight toward us. Dad's head shot around to check my position, and he probably shouted something, but if he did, I didn't hear it.

Despite my lack of comfort riding in traffic, my six years of off-roading suddenly kicked in. Countless times, while riding fast through the forests and swamps of Florida, I had rounded a bend and was surprised by the unexpected in my path, including armadillos, alligators, fallen trees, and sometimes another dirt biker closing fast from the opposite direction. The decision needed to be instant; do I hit the object blocking the trail and try to ride it out, or do I point the bike toward something further away then try to stop before hitting this new target? Within a blink, I, too, dove my bike hard to the right where spectators lining the curb scattered. I skidded to a stop as my front wheel jumped the curb. The racecars flew past just a few feet behind our rear fenders.

Before Dad and I could even check on one another, we were met by a policeman shouting at us in Greek. Dad put a hand up, signaling me to sit still and to keep my mouth shut.

The policeman spoke no English, and apparently, neither did any of the agitated bystanders freely opining on our sudden entrance into the race. The policeman stretched an open palm to me and uttered what sounded like "li-seens." I shrugged and looked to Dad who pulled out his wallet and handed the official his driver's license and passport. There may have been a few Drachmas also handed over, but I can't be sure. I only know that the frustrated policeman soon shook his head, threw up his arms, and directed us through an alley that led away from the makeshift racecourse. Within minutes, we were again on our way, leaving town on the road northwest toward Athens.

Dad once again took the lead, but with the town disappearing in our rearview mirrors, he chopped his throttle and waved me forward to ride alongside. He turned his head to me and raised his hand to form a questioning, "OK?" I nodded my head, raised my left fist, and offered my thumbs-up. It was the signal that this "King Aegeus" was looking for, and he was satisfied that his boy was unshaken and still with him, Dad twisted the right grip and resumed the lead.

I couldn't suppress a slight grin as we motored along this birthplace of mythology and land of heroic legend. This was my first road trip as commander of my own motorcycle, and I had already acquired a fantastic tale to call my very own. A tale that required a rendezvous with the unexpected.

At 5:00 p.m. Vegas time, my bike was fully loaded. She was as prepped as I could make her. I gave Kim and the twins a big squeeze, climbed aboard the Beemer, and headed to Trent's place.

I was the first to arrive, but I was soon joined by my brother-in-law, Steve, on his BMW and my friend, Don, on his Ducati Multistrada. Trent was held up at work but arrived around 5:45. The part he had expected for the Buell had arrived that afternoon, and he handed it to me as he ran upstairs to change into his riding gear. Don, Steve, and I installed the part that I prayed would cure the engine computer problems. The touted solution was an air flow diverter that mounted over the exhaust system to shield the sensors from the exhaust heat and bring cooler air to the rear cylinder. I remained frustrated that this problem was not already rectified and that we were starting the journey with uncertainty.

Twenty minutes later, we all mounted up to head to Laughlin. At the first stop sign, I jumped off my bike to take a quick photo before hitting the road.

Friday evening traffic in the Las Vegas valley makes for slow progress, but we made our way east through Henderson to finally exit the valley at Railroad Pass. We then turned south on U.S. 95 for the 90-mile ride to Lake Mojave and Laughlin.

Thirty minutes down the road, as the highway skirted alongside a dry lakebed, I saw a narrow ribbon of blacktop descending the valley from the eastern hills to tee into 95 just in front of us. I recognized it as the road to Nelson's Landing. I smiled; I'll never forget that road.

———

Back in 1988, one of my riding buddies was friends with a producer of television commercials who, at the time, was making a TV spot for the Rio Hotel and Casino in Las Vegas. It seemed that he needed some old-school motorcycles and some riders who could handle a unique assignment: dress up as animal characters (think of the suits worn by college mascots) and ride our motorcycles in tight formation to accompany "Rio Rita" as she rumbled into Vegas for a weekend of fun at the Rio. A few weeks later, early on a July morning, I found myself on a wide spot on Nelson's Landing Road, surrounded by cameras, RVs, and caterers while I was outfitted in an eagle suit, complete with a giant fiberglass head. My fellow riders were, likewise, adorned in mascot suits– pandas, lizards, a piggy, and a chef. We could only see out through a small screen in the neck of the suits, and the heads would nearly blow off our shoulders as we gained speed. Riding in formation on a narrow road is particularly challenging when you can't see left nor right, and the tiny viewing window dances around from the wind. That was the closest I'd ever come to knowing what it feels like to be a pilot for the Blue Angels or Thunderbirds, taking care of doing your own part and trusting those around you to do theirs. It was a unique experience to be sure, and I smiled to myself as Trent, Steve, Don and I rolled past this now vacant desert road.

US 95 runs a beeline through a broad desert valley, and we kept our speed at 80 and above. It had not been a hot day, but I kept an eye on Trent, watching for signs of overheating trouble from his Buell. The sun set as we rode through Searchlight, and it was complete darkness by the time we turned east on Highway 163 to descend from the high desert to Davis Dam on the Colorado River. Route 163 was broad and newly paved, with long sweepers that snaked through the hills. I had taken the lead once we turned off 95, and Don was tight on my tail. It seemed that Don and his Ducati wanted to push me through the curves to see what the Beemer could do. We hit those twisties hard but stayed close together through them all.

We arrived in Laughlin a little after 9:00 and had dinner at In-and-Out Burger, a treat we didn't get back in North Carolina. Trent reported no troubles from the Buell, but I still wondered how it would do in elevated temperatures and after many hours of high-speed riding.

Don visited with us for a while then rode away to return to Vegas, while Trent, Steve, and I headed to The Tropicana Hotel/Casino to bunk for the night. We parked our bikes in the parking garage and toted our gear a *loooong* way to our room. I checked into our Facebook group and reported that we were in place at the starting line and set for launch in the morning. We received well-wishes and many cautions to "be careful" from as far away as South Africa, the Philippines, Australia, and Scotland. At 11:00, we called it a night.

It was then that I made a bone-headed error. Perhaps it was the late hour, but there really was not an excuse. I had planned to rise at 5:00 a.m. to get a jump on the day, but we were getting to bed a bit later than I'd planned. For some reason, I got my time zone calculations backward; I decided at the last minute that we could set the alarm for 6:00 a.m. Pacific Time, since (I figured) that would be the equivalent of 5:00 a.m. Mountain Time, which is where we would spend the majority of the day on Saturday. In reality, 6:00 a.m. Pacific Time is the equivalent of 7:00 a.m. Mountain Time and so my late-night error would cost us valuable miles in the coming day.

Steve laid a sleeping bag on the floor while Trent and I took the beds. Saturday would begin the adventure of our lives, and the first day was slated to be a thousand-mile ride, so we needed our rest. We exchanged a few comments after the lights went out, followed by silence.

CHAPTER 8
DAY ONE
SATURDAY, MAY 27TH

We arose a little before six PDT and got set for the day: chaps on, sunscreen applied, head bandanna wetted (serves as a "swamp cooler" under the helmet) and morning prayer offered. We were fully aware that our safety does not wholly lie within our own hands and that we needed the grace from the *Man Upstairs* to care for us where we cannot care for ourselves. Prayer was a consistent part of our morning routine.

Packed and ready, we were out the door by six-fifteen. We loaded the bikes and rode to a Terrible Herbst gas station that was already busy with a number of weekend boaters who were getting set for a day on the river. We filled our Camelbacks with Gatorade and our gas tanks with premium and set our odometers to zero. It was 6:31 a.m. We would have 240 hours until 7:31 a.m. MDT on Tuesday, June 6th to complete the ride when we cross the northern Idaho/Utah border on I-84 near Snowville to collect our 48th state.

We rolled out of that Laughlin gas station, quickly crossed the bridge over the Colorado River to enter Arizona, and I smiled. *That's two states in two minutes*, I thought. We continued south on US 95 through Bullhead City as the sun rose into a clear blue sky. We followed the Colorado for 32 miles to Needles, California, and grabbed a quick breakfast sandwich at McDonalds.

Because Steve would only be riding with us for half the day, Trent let him borrow his helmet radio headset so that Steve and I could communicate until he had to turn around to head back to Vegas.

Although Steve's plan to ride 500 miles with us before heading back toward Las Vegas was quite ambitious for a newcomer to distance-riding, Steve has always wanted to be a part of whatever was going on, and he's proven aggressive at attacking his goals.

In Needles, we took the onramp to I-40 eastbound which would be our home for most of the day.

Interstates are my least-favorite routes for riding a motorcycle. They cover the terrain while missing the country. They are the Cliffs-Notes of terrestrial travel, giving you only a general idea of this nation by hurriedly bypassing the rich colors of community and by speed-reading through the stories that deserve contemplation, both the anthropological and the geographical. Yes, I-40 has its points of beauty as it climbs from the junipers of the Mojave Desert into the dark pines of Flagstaff and then descends again to the arid lands of Winslow, but I can't help but mourn as I ride past the Highway 89 exit sign at Ash Fork. I know it leads to the mining town of Jerome, with its old homes and frontier business establishments, clinging like ivy to the steep mountainside. I shake my head as I roll past the Williams exit as it offers no clue to the Route 66 charm of this gateway to the Grand Canyon. I also know where to get off the freeway near Flagstaff to enjoy the splendor of Oak Creek Canyon, Slide Rock, and Sedona. You can't go fast through any of those places, nor would you want to. If you did, these places might not go through you.

I recalled riding through many years ago with my buddy, Scott Doney, as we turned north to ride through the Navajo Indian reservation and on to the North Rim of the Grand Canyon. I smiled at the recollection of one gas stop in particular on that ride.

They call it the Arizona Strip. It consists of the portion of north-western Arizona cut off from the rest of the state by the Grand Canyon and its vistas call to memory every John Ford western ever made. Scott and I had crossed the Colorado River at Navajo Bridge to traverse the Arizona strip on Highway 89 on our way back to Las Vegas.

We stopped for gas in a dusty desert town at an old '50s style gas station seemingly frozen in time, showing no signs of modernity–just a pair of old-school pumps (one regular, one hi-test) and neither took credit cards. The grease racks in the two repair bays stood vacant. A small office offered nothing more to purchase than a selection of faded

Texaco maps, and the restrooms located around the side were small, well-worn, but clean.

In country towns such as this, they often let you pump your gas before settling up with the proprietor. I topped the tank on my BMW R100RT, went inside to pay the attendant, then made use of the facilities for a quick bio-break. When I returned to the pumps, Scott had finished fueling his Beemer and was poring over an atlas he had retrieved from his rear box. We both agreed to turn off on Highway 389 to take in Pipe Springs on our way to Hurricane, Utah, then we'd shoot south on I-15 to Vegas. We mounted up and headed out.

I was riding lead, when some distance west of Fredonia, I heard Scott's horn blow repeatedly as he accelerated to come up on my left. The face shield to his helmet was raised and he appeared ashen and alarmed. He motioned me to pull over, and I suspected something was seriously wrong. I found a broad spot on the shoulder and brought my bike to a stop as Scott pulled to a halt next to me. His brow was bent in deep concern.

"I didn't pay for my gas!" he shouted over the idling motors. "Back in Fredonia–I forgot to pay the attendant when I fueled up!"

Over the years, I had ridden more miles with Scott Doney than with anyone outside of my own family. I knew the man, and I knew his integrity. I didn't need to ask him what he wanted to do. I simply nodded my head and motioned for him to take lead. He spun his bike around, and I followed him east to Fredonia.

It was a surprised proprietor who accepted Scott's payment, quite some time after this biker had inadvertently stiffed him for less than four dollars' worth of gas. We mounted back up and rode toward the sinking sun.

As we motored along, I thought how good it was that there were still men like my friend Scott. Honor-bound. Duty-bound. Honest and true whether it be to friends or to strangers. I will never forget that distraught look on his face as he rode up beside me earlier that day. It was nobility personified in true manliness, in solid grit and character. I thought it ironic that there are many who could not be tempted to abandon their integrity for a million dollars, yet there are few like Scott who, despite the fact he owed but a pittance and against the popular notion that when we stiff a *business*, we are not really harming *people*, Scott's honor could not be purchased for pocket change. That lowly, seemingly insignificant level is where most men fail and where integrity is put to the test.

I saw once again that the open road brings far more than transient scenery and short-lived thrills. The journey invites opportunity and tempts God and His angels to put in our path experiences that can remain with us long after the engines have cooled, and the bedrolls have been shoved back up into the rafters. Sure, the odometer stops, but the ride remains.

My mind returned from those side roads I love so well to that efficient bisector of the Southwest known as I-40. On this day – on this trip – I reluctantly acknowledged that the interstate is my friend, or at least an acquaintance with utility, as we blasted across the Grand Canyon State.

Sometime in the mid-morning, Steve reported over the radio that his right wrist was really getting sore from holding the throttle open. I knew his bike was too old and too spartan to feature an electronic cruise control, so I asked him if there was a thumbscrew or a friction screw somewhere on the right-side controls that could be tightened to hold the throttle in position, allowing relief from the throttle return spring. This thumbscrew can be found on some of my older bikes and can really be a wrist-saver on long rides, but Steve wasn't able to find one on his Beemer.

We stopped for fuel at Seligman, and I traded bikes with Steve. I knew from having test-ridden his motorcycle in Las Vegas that this would not be a comfortable mount for riding long distance, so I had planned on letting him ride my bike for part of the day anyway. However, I was not prepared for the cramp-inducing resistance I found from that right grip when I hit the highway on Steve's R/S. Gold's Gym does not feature isometric devices to match this monster! After a while, I even tried using my left hand on the right grip to hold the throttle open, but as any of you who have tried that trick can attest, that was a bad idea. The brain does not quickly adjust muscle memory, and I found myself steering *backward*–drifting left when I wanted to correct to the right and visa-versa. I continued on, locked into an unalterable forward-leaning riding position, my right fist straining to keep the throttle open and my left hand covering my right forearm to massage the throbbing muscle.

In Flagstaff, I traded bikes with Trent–he rode the "Hand grip from Hell," I took over the Buell, and Steve remained on my Beemer. We pulled off at Winslow, not only for gas, but I wanted to show the boys that famous "corner in Winslow Arizona that's such a fine sight to see," from the Eagles song "Taking in Easy." We shot a few photos on the downtown corner where the City of Winslow has recreated the lyrical scene complete with an old "flatbed Ford".

| Trent and me on the corner in Winslow

We then rode back to the interstate and gassed up while a long line of at least thirty Harleys were also drinking in petrol at the pumps. There were chase vans accompanying these bikes, and one of the riders from the group came over to chat. He was from South Africa, and he was a client of this organized motorcycle tour company, specializing in covering the entire Route 66. The man ran a motorcycle tour company of his own in Namibia. I laid a little Afrikaans on him (from my days down in South Africa), but I think I spoke the language better than he did.

We continued east to Gallup where we arrived around 3:30. It was then that I realized I'd screwed up my time zone calculations, and we were really running behind schedule, having only covered 430 miles. Our target for the night was Johnson City, Kansas, and we were now projected to arrive well after midnight. I encouraged Steve to turn around and head home from Gallup, but he was determined to ride 500 miles with us before heading back, and he stayed with us.

We rode on to Albuquerque where we hit the 500-mile mark and pulled off at an exit to wish Steve Godspeed as he turned around for Vegas, promising to stop if he got too tired and to keep us informed of his progress via text message. I was very concerned for Steve and watched my phone closely for the rest of the day and night.

Trent and I gassed again at Cline's Corners and continued east on I-40. By the time we got to Santa Rosa, the night had brought quite the windstorm, complete with what we later learned to be tornadic activity in the area. The rain came and the side gusts were so bad we had a hard time keeping the bikes on the highway. We rode with the bikes leaned into the wind. When we passed on the leeward side of tractor trailers, the wind was momentarily blocked. The bikes, suddenly relieved of the side-drafts, dove toward the trucks forcing us to quickly correct to keep from making contact.

As we approached Tucumcari, conditions had only gotten worse. Rain made visibility low and the semi's seemed to be fighting to remain upright. I called an end to our efforts for the day, and we pulled into an old Route 66 motel in Tucumcari at 9:30 with only four states under our belts and just 729 miles covered, (271 miles short of our goal).

The motel had no restaurant, and it was storming too severely for us to ride to find dinner, so we ate fare from our saddlebags. The motel room qualified as a fleabag and there were almost no other guests, judging from the near-empty parking lot.

I switched on the desk lamp and opened the road atlas. I was frustrated that we didn't start the day earlier and that we had to end the day too soon due to weather. We needed over 800 miles per day, and we knew that any shortfall must be made up for on another day. We checked the weather reports and learned of the tornadoes that had touched down in the area. Worse yet, our route for day two would head straight into the teeth of the storm system. I expressed my discouragement out loud as I pored over the road atlas. This is when Trent showed a trait he would maintain throughout the odyssey; he simply did not share my level of anxiety over our schedule. "We'll be alright, Dad–things will work out."

I reported to our Facebook group and received messages of encouragement from our followers. Many said they were praying for our safety, and all expressed support for our decision to take shelter rather than battle the storm.

I repeatedly checked the phone for a message from Steve, worried that he would push himself too far in his determination to capture a 1000-mile day.

I had made suggestions to Steve that he turn back toward home as early as Flagstaff. I assured him that he had nothing to prove. Every time I encouraged him to peel off and head home, he declined, saying he wanted to ride with us for 500 miles before he headed back home. When we parted, I asked him to promise that he would only go as far as Kingman. He said, "We'll see," with little attempt at sincerity. I encouraged him to pull over and camp in the desert if he got sleepy, and he promised to do so. I also asked him to text us at each gas stop because I was going to worry about him until I knew he was done riding for the day.

We received texts from Steve through the night. He fueled in Sanders, AZ, then again in Flagstaff. He fueled in Kingman at 12:53 in the morning and indicated he was continuing on. I then got another text from him that read:

Steve: Man, I have to stop for rest. Everything hurts. It took me five minutes to get off the bike. I had a chance to stand during slow traffic, and I couldn't stand.
I felt like Rocky Balboa's cornerman begging him to stay down; he had nothing more to prove.
Me: I hate to see you press on just for a cheap certificate (from The Iron Butt Association). Staying alive is more important.
Steve: Not a problem staying awake; just moving.

His next text came at 3:36 in the morning.
Steve: Home.
Me: Wow! That's an Iron Will

CHAPTER 9
DAY TWO
SUNDAY, MAY 28TH

We woke before sunrise to a calmer day and noticed, in the dawning light, that there was an enormous windmill/generator directly over our motel. I commented that this must be the reason why it was so windy last night– they probably had that thing turned on too high. Trent rolled his eyes and muttered, "Dad jokes..."

We rolled through Tucumcari, which is a stereotypical Route 66 town that appeared to be stuck in the 1950s. Old motels and service stations seemed to be right out of one of Disney's *Cars* movies. Today's agenda didn't call for interstate highways, rather, it kept us on US routes and state highways as we aimed to just clip the northwest corner of the Texas panhandle before riding due north through the slim panhandle of Oklahoma, continuing north into the southeast corner of Colorado. From there, it would be due east across southern Kansas and Missouri.

We headed up US-54 for Dalhart, Texas, where we gassed at a convenience market and chatted with some Harley dresser riders out for a Sunday ride. They were astonished to know that we had just left Nevada the previous morning and aimed to be at the Mississippi River by day's end.

We switched bikes between the two of us, a practice we would continue for much of the trip. This helped us remain fresh as the ergonomics on the two bikes were quite different and offered a welcome change or, at least, it varied the parts that were getting numbed. Whoever had the Beemer would take lead since it had the

GPS and the cruise control to set the pace. As we rode, we remained in contact via our helmet-to-helmet radios, but these tended to lose their charge after eight hours or so. We brought along rechargeable auxiliary batteries that we could plug into our headsets once they lost power, and those would usually carry us well into the night. Our motel nightstands tended to be quite the rat's-nest of chargers for our phones, radios, and auxiliary battery packs.

We also pre-planned our gas stops to maximize efficiency (like a NASCAR pit crew). One of us would gas the bikes while the other ran into the station to re-wet our doo-rags or refill our Camelbacks. If one guy had to use the restroom, the other guy was the "gasman" on that stop to save time.

We intended to take US-385 north out of Dalhart but ended up on US-87 by mistake heading northwest. After 30 minutes or so, we discovered our error and found an unmarked, desolate, but paved road that led east toward 385. This was one of the most memorable roads of the trip; it went straight as an arrow across the flattest West Texas sagebrush country, occasionally passing an abandoned ranch house. Every few miles, the road would make a 90-degree turn to the north, followed a few miles later by a 90-degree turn back to the east. We never saw another car the entire time on this road, and we hit some pretty high speeds as we tried to make up for lost time.

We found Hwy 385 and continued north to cross the panhandle of Oklahoma, getting a gas receipt in Boise City. We crossed into Colorado and stopped for another receipt in Campo before turning east on US-160 to roll on into Kansas. As we passed Johnson City, I thought about the fact that this was supposed to have been our endpoint for day one, and this was a good gauge for how far behind we were.

The high winds from the previous night had moved east across the Great Plains, but the dark clouds in front of us indicated we were catching up with the storm. Just west of Ulysses, Kansas, we were pulled over by a Kansas Highway Patrol officer who noticed our speed (85

mph in a 65 zone). He was a friendly and chatty guy who was very interested in the story of our 48-state ride and of the veterans' cause we were associated with. He told us quite a bit about the history of the area, and he was particularly proud of the grain production in that part of the country. I was torn between wanting to be nice to this officer in hopes that we could avoid a ticket and just wanting him to shut up and write the citation. Trent was his usual nonchalant self, and he even grinned into his cell phone as he took a selfie photo of the squad car behind our bikes. I warned him not to get too cheeky, but that breath is wasted on Trent.

The patrolman warned us of bad tornadic activity if we continue on 160 through southern Kansas and Missouri. He strongly suggested we would be better off to shoot north to I-70. This would add a couple hundred miles to our trip, but it would likely be as fast (and far safer) than proceeding into this storm–a storm that ended up being a doozy. By the time it went through Missouri and into Memphis it was one of the worst storms in recent years for that area. It was likely a great blessing that the trooper pulled us over, or we would have continued into the teeth of that storm. We were let off with a warning (no ticket) and continued east to Dodge City, then north to connect with I-70 just west of Salina.

We avoided bad weather, though it was perpetually overcast, and I kept an eye out for that spot on I-70, 20 miles west of Topeka, where my brother, Jeff, and I were in the accident that nearly ended our lives and that permanently took the hearing from my right ear. I was unable to identify the exact spot but saw a couple of places that fit my memory of the site.

As we passed grain silo after grain silo, I had to chuckle. I keyed the radio and spoke with Trent, "You know that your Grandpa Jim grew up near here. As a matter of fact, he once told me that he earned extra money in college by tying a broom to the back fender of his Harley and sweeping out grain silos for farmers by riding round and round inside the silos, up and down the walls."

Trent responded, "Yeah, right!"

I continued, "Dad said this worked out really well for him until one day when he came out the top of a silo."

My dad was full of tall tales, and the problem was, some of them were true!

We continued east into Missouri, riding past the Truman Sports Complex (Go Chiefs and Royals!) at Raytown as we kept pressing eastward in the darkness, making good time on I-70 where we could keep our speed elevated with little worry of "over-driving our head-lights" to find surprises appear before us on the darkened road. Nocturnal surprises can put you down hard!

———

On their 1953 ride to Veracruz, Mexico, Dad and his buddy, Gene Clampett, rode identical Harley Hydra-Glides. Late one evening, a few hundred miles into Mexico, they were riding side-by-side at 70 mph when their headlights revealed a barricade fully stretching across the road to warn of a washed-out bridge. Dad hit his brakes and dove his sickle off the road to the right, while Clampett peeled off the road to the left. Dad said his Harley pitched and bucked over rocks before he separated from the bike as man and machine tumbled into, and through, a camp of construction workers for the bridge repairs. Dad said the men scattered fast as first the motorcycle and then the rider came bouncing past their campfire.

Dad was scraped up a bit, and the Harley lost a left spotlight but was otherwise in good shape. Dad limped up to the road and to the other side to check on Clampett, who was just then getting his Harley restarted. Clampett's Hog was also now missing its left spotlight; remarkably, both bikes sustained nearly identical battle scars and remained each other's twin.

Dad and Clampett laid out their bedrolls with the Mexicans, and in the morning, they faced a unique challenge in crossing the river. The workers had built a temporary pontoon bridge made up of two dozen rowboats tied side-by-side and onto which they had fastened two rows of planks across the bows and sterns that served as the bridge for cars to cross the river. This worked well for four wheeled vehicles that are laterally stable, but it proved tricky for two-wheeled motorcycles. To keep the boats from tipping from the weight of just one motorcycle, Dad and Clampett had to ride across these planks at the same time, side-by-side, dabbing their feet down onto the gunwales of the rowboats from time to time to keep their balance.

Dad reported that it was quite the challenge as the boats bobbed under the weight of the bikes. He and Clampett had to stay dead-even with one another, and they couldn't afford to miss finding the gunwales with a foot or they'd have rolled off into the river. Dad says that when they reached the far bank, their newly made Mexican friends let out quite the cheer. The two riders then continued on to Veracruz where they found a Harley dealer and replaced the spotlights. No major marks remained on the motorcycles, but the memory of the washed-out bridge, of camping with the Mexicans, and of riding Harleys over rowboats would mark both men's memories for decades to come.

This photo is from that trip and that's my dad sitting on his Harley at the Mexican border.

At 11:30, after 17 hours of riding, Trent and I finally pulled off the interstate at Odessa Missouri, to get some sleep.

We had started the day in New Mexico and had collected Texas, Oklahoma, Colorado, Kansas, and Missouri that day, but I was still upset. We should have been to the Mississippi River by now, and we were at least half a day behind schedule. The Buell's misfiring issue seemed to be resolved, but it was now leaking fork fluid which ran down the front forks to saturate the brake pads, rendering the front brakes nearly useless. I'd also noticed that the BMW was requiring an unusual amount of handlebar input to maintain a straight line on the highway. It wasn't a high amount of effort, rather a high frequency of corrections; kind of like a truck with an over-tightened steering gearbox (if any of you readers are old enough to know what I'm talking about here). Anyway, I noticed that the rear tire on the BMW was wearing very flat and square across the center section, and I wondered if that was causing the stability issue. I adjusted the air pressure but noticed little improvement. I hoped that the upcoming change of tires I planned for in Charlotte would fix the problem. It wasn't dangerous; just annoying and something I'm certainly not accustomed to on the Harley. Big Red rode on rails and never wandered until I told it to do so.

CHAPTER 10
DAY THREE

MONDAY, MAY 29TH

We rose before sunrise, intending to make this a big *catch-up* day for miles captured. We gassed up and hit I-70 toward St. Louis on a clear day that held great promise with no issues other than growing concerns about the saturated brake pads on the Buell. I had Bluetooth phone service in my helmet, and I called one of my coworkers back home in Charlotte to see if he could find a Harley shop in the area with hopes that they could order in the fork seals and brake pads. I figured that we could have those replaced while I have the tires installed on the Beemer. My friend found a dealer in Statesville who could order the parts overnight to be ready for us on Tuesday, understanding the time-crunch we were under on this Iron Butt challenge. We tied some rags around the Buell's fork seals to serve as *diapers* to prevent more oil from flowing down to the brake pads.

We avoided St. Louis traffic by turning south on I-55 toward Cape Girardeau. As we passed the signs that pointed toward St. Charles, my mind returned to the father/son ride of 1974 when we stopped here for Dad to meet up again with his old riding buddy, Gene Clampett, who he had not seen in nearly twenty years. As referenced before, the stories of Dad and Gene were legendary in the Stephenson household.

———

There was that time when Dad and Gene did their skinny-dip in that cow pasture. There was the incident Dad told of when he and Gene rode into downtown Cheyanne and dismounted their motorcycles among a crowd of local cowboys outside of a bar. Gene tossed off his jacket, tilted back his head, and shouted, "Somebody grease this town and I'll swallow it!"

Though, to this day, I don't understand what Gene meant by that. Dad said that the locals seemed to understand that this barrel-chested biker was ready to challenge anyone and there was none who stepped forward to oblige.

The stories were tall, and the adventures were grand when Clampett's name was part of the tale, and I looked forward to finally meeting him on that evening in '74 when Dad and I pulled our motorcycles into a vacant shopping center parking lot in St. Charles. Dad found a pay phone. He flipped through the pages of the phone book, then he dropped a dime in the slot and dialed the number. A few minutes later, Dad hung up and said, "Gene's coming over to meet us here."

Gene and Dad in gag photo.

| Gene and "Slim" stop for refreshment in 1953.

Twenty minutes later, we stood by our motorcycles when a low thunder grew louder. We then saw a headlight approach the turn-in to the shopping center. As Gene wheeled his Hog into the drive, both of his legs were splayed straight out and his head was rocked back as he let out a, "HAW, HAW, HAW!"

He rocked his old Harley left then right as he approached, the footboards tossing sparks from contact with the asphalt. He pulled to a stop right next to us, and with one continuous motion, his left foot extended his sidestand, his right hand went to the tank to switch off the motor, and he leaped from the saddle to greet Dad in a bear hug. "How ya doin', Slim! Geez it's great to see you!"

He was all that I'd expected, even with a bare pate and a belly that had grown to match his broad shoulders. It was a treat to sit back and listen to these two old trail-mates catch up and reminisce. I looked over his motorcycle–a red and white late-'50s Duo Glide– something right out of the stories I'd heard from childhood. What a perfect evening.

Years later, in the mid-1990s Dad rode his "Big Red" 1990 Harley

Electra Glide to St. Charles, and again visited his old friend. Gene still rode the same bike.

| My brother Steve got to ride a bit with Dad and Gene.

Trent and I hit Cape Girardeau and crossed the Mississippi into Illinois, getting gas in Olive Branch, at a rustic old gas station/tire shop straight out of the Great Depression. It was charming, but I was reminded how much better we have it as motorist these days. There was a time, particularly in the '40s and '50s, when service stations were closed by nine or ten o'clock at night. If you wanted to ride late into the evening, you either needed to top off your tanks by closing time or carry an extra can of gas on the back fender.

As we filled our tanks, I related a story my dad told me about an evening when he and some of his riding buddies were heading back to Fayetteville, Arkansas, from the dirt track races in Springfield, Missouri. They rode state highways that only passed through small farm towns with apparently early bedtime habits. By eight o'clock in the evening, they were unable to find an open gas station in any of the little towns they rode through. They pressed on, thinking that, surely, there would be an open station in the next town. The evening grew late, and a few of the sickles coughed and sputtered before being switched to their reserve tanks. That's when dad had an idea.

Dad had worked at a filling station during high school, and he knew that there was always a couple of pints of fuel in the loop of the gas hose that hung down between the filler nozzle and the pump. For the rest of the evening, at every station they came across, Dad and his buddies would drain these remnants from the hose on every pump. Since motorcycles don't require a great deal of gas per mile ridden, they were able to nurse their sickles, small sips at a time, all the way back to Fayetteville, arriving well after midnight. In this day of 24-hour stations, the riding experience is not exactly the same as it was in those earlier days when the lack of conveniences called for an increase in ingenuity.

We continued south along a scenic river drive to Fulton, Kentucky, where we stopped for a cold Frosty at a Wendy's. Some big ol' boy in overalls and no shirt sat near us in the restaurant, and out of the blue, he talked to us about his motorcycle riding days. Trent later commented that folks in the south didn't even wait until you make eye contact to initiate a conversation. Certainly, a sign of southern hospitality but kind of strange if you're not used to it.

We crossed back over to the western bank of the Mississippi to take in Arkansas and took gas in Blythville. I regretted that our route would touch only briefly in Arkansas, a state that featured so prominently in the stories my dad told us of his early years as a rider.

It was while he was a student at the University of Arkansas that Dad and his riding buddies used to hang out at a bar across the street from the police station. Next to the police station sat the dog pound. One night, on a dare, Dad chained the gates of the dog pound to the rear bumper of a patrol car sitting in front of the station. When a police officer came out and headed off on patrol, his car pulled down the gates of the pound and released a dozen hounds onto the streets of Fayetteville.

It was on Arkansas Route 65 that Bob Hunt, riding solo, stopped for gas at a remote service station and found a bold way to get out of a threatening situation. After topping his fuel tank, Bob had gone into the men's room and, upon returning to his Hog, he found a beefy country boy in his mid twenties sitting on his bike; three of the big man's buddies stood off to the side.

"Nice motorsickle," drawled the redneck as his hands went to the grips. "You don't mind if I take it for a spin, do you?" The man winked at his buddies who smirked and nudged one another with their elbows.

Bob never slowed his pace. He walked behind the Harley and straight up to the gas pump. He retrieved the nozzle with his right hand, flipped a switch with his left before reaching into the left pocket of his jacket, retrieving a Zippo lighter. Without a word, Bob gave the nozzle a squeeze as he swept downward to drench the man's left side from shoulder to ankle in gasoline.

The old boy let out with a string of curse words as his buddies charged toward Bob – but the cursing ceased, and everyone froze when Bob flipped open the Zippo and held it next to the big man's ear.

Bob spoke low and slow as the man's wide eyes stared at the lighter. "Turn the switch on the tank one click to the right, then put your right foot to the starter pedal, and start kicking–and pray she don't backfire!"

The man did as instructed, and the already-warm engine fired up on the first kick. Bob had the man dismount toward him and the pale hillbilly slowly shuffled toward the rear of the bike. Bob gave the nozzle another squeeze and set the lock to keep the flow going. The man took off in a run as Bob slid the hose along the concrete behind the bike. One of the three other men went to capture the loose gas hose as Bob jumped into the saddle, stomped the bike into gear, and blew out of that gas station like a rifle shot. If those hicks had the nerve to take chase, Bob never saw sign of them in his mirrors.

These, and many more such stories, call me to ride the roads of Arkansas in search of those places I've seen so clearly in my mind that I'd swear I'd recognize them even though I've never before been to those sites. Not on this ride – perhaps another time soon.

The storm that we chased through Kansas, then avoided with our loop up to I-70, had slowly soaked the Ozarks before hitting the Mississippi River and turning south toward the Gulf of Mexico; we were once again gaining on the tempest. We crossed back over the Mississippi at Memphis and headed south on I-55. We caught up with the rain showers as soon as we hit Mississippi, and it got thick quick, making it nearly impossible to see much distance and slowing us down considerably. We donned our rain gear, and the Buell revealed how limited the protection was from its tiny windshield as the rain pretty well hit the rider directly. The brakes, already a problem on that bike, were even worse in the rain.

We stopped for gas around noon and enjoyed the shelter of the truck stop canopies while we fueled and ate some food. Many motorists were likewise taking a break from the drenching downpour; it was no fun to drive in, even in a car. We had been stopped for probably 25 minutes before we decided that the rain wasn't going to let up, and we determined to charge back into the storm.

When we went to start the bikes, the Buell wouldn't fire. Trent had inadvertently left the ignition switch on (and therefore the headlights), and the battery was now too weak to start the bike.

I told Trent to put the bike in second gear and I'd give him a push to see if we could bump-start the bike. I pushed for all I was worth in the driving rain, and Trent dumped the clutch, but the back tire only slid on the wet pavement. I instructed Trent to try third gear where we would get less slippage; we only needed the cylinders to fire once, and we'd be in business. I told him that I was only good for one more strong effort pushing this 600 lb. bike and rider. We gave it a go; I put my shoulder into the rear pack and drove the bike forward, and Trent again dumped the clutch. The motor turned over once before the rear tire again locked, and the bike didn't start.

Then Trent said, "Oops."

I could see his grin even through the rain on his helmet's face shield. "I forgot to change the kill switch to the 'run' position," he offered sheepishly.

If I had had any energy left, I would have added a new meaning to the term "kill switch."

We pushed the bike back to the canopy, and I went into the truck stop to try to buy or borrow a set of jumper cables. Surprisingly, the truck stop didn't have any. Their mechanic was away at the time, so they couldn't tell me if he had any cables I could borrow to jump the Buell with the Beemer. There was another truck stop on the other side of the road, so I sloshed my way over there and found a set of cables I could purchase. I returned, and we were able to fire up the Buell and resume our ride, but we had consumed over one hour of precious riding time. That meant we were an additional 80 miles behind schedule.

With the weather challenges slowing us down, it was apparent we would not be finishing the day anywhere near Charlotte. So, I called ahead to let the BMW dealer know that we wouldn't be in for those tires until Wednesday morning. They said they would be ready to hustle on the change-out.

The rain never let up the entire day and night, and the roads were so overrun with water that Trent commented that we'd make better time if we were riding jet skis.

I remained in the lead for the rest of the afternoon and evening, and I kept a constant eye on my mirrors to make certain that Trent's headlight was still with me. It was often hard to see him through the rain.

It had been one of the surprises that came with being a parent; activities that I have never worried about when it came to my own involvement (like riding motorcycles) became a point of concern once my own kids engaged in the sport. I've always felt like I had good control over my own fate out on the road, but I fretted mightily over what I knew could happen to my children, feeling the heavy responsibility for drawing them into an often-hazardous pursuit.

————

When our oldest daughter, Jillian, was in college, she decided to get her motorcycle license. I loaned her a Suzuki Intruder 800 to practice on, and in a short time, she had passed all riding tests and obtained her motorcycle endorsement.

The following summer, she and I planned to ride the two bikes (me on my Electra Glide and she on the Intruder) from our Southern Utah home, across the Great Basin, and into Yosemite National Park in California. We left early one June morning rolling west on Utah 56 into Panaca, Nevada, before turning south on US-93 to pass through Caliente.

The far side of Caliente is dressed in low hills with moderate curves. I was riding lead as we negotiated the mid-speed sweepers. After a series of four or five of these curves, I noticed that Jill was no longer in my mirrors, and I slowed for her to catch up. When her headlight didn't appear, I pulled over to wait. After only thirty seconds or so, I knew there was trouble. I spun the bike around and charged back up the highway.

As I rode, I noticed there were no cars now coming around these curves toward me and chills shot up my spine.

I rounded a left-hand sweeper and saw three or four cars had stopped and pulled to both sides of the road. My heart twisted within my chest. I scanned the shoulders for signs of Jill's motorcycle but saw nothing. As I approached, I could see men down in a depression on the left side of the road, their attention riveted on something in the brush. And then, among the rocks and Joshua trees, I spotted the motorcycle – windshield shattered, gear scattered, metal bent.

My eyes were fixed on the scene down in the draw as I stopped the Harley and dismounted. As I crossed the road, my eyes searched among the debris for a sign of my daughter, but she wasn't there. As I reached the far shoulder, I heard her voice, "Dad!"

I turned to the right and saw Jillian leaning against the hood of a car with a kind man attending to her. She still had on her helmet. Her jacket and pants were torn and caked in dust.

I ran to her, "Jill, are you alright?"

"I think so," she replied as she tried to stand up straight. She immediately fell back against the hood of the car.

"Take it easy, honey; where do you hurt?"

"I don't know–I–Dad, I can't see."

I swallowed my panic. I had recently read in the papers the account of a celebrity involved in a rollover accident outside of Las Vegas. He had emerged from the wreckage complaining of dizziness and loss of vision. Before the ambulance arrived, the man had perished from head trauma.

"What do you mean you can't see?"

Her eyes darted about, and she didn't respond.

I asked the man who had attended to her if he would drive us into Caliente "Right NOW!" I was not going to wait for an ambulance. Leaving my bike and her bike on the side of the road, I loaded Jill into his backseat, and we took off.

I tried to keep her talking as we rushed toward town.

"Sorry, Dad–I ran off the road."

"It's okay, Jill–now tell me what you're feeling."

"I'm starting to see okay. Everything else hurts."

We got to the medical center in Caliente, such as it was, and the staff assessed Jill's condition. I kept telling them about her vision troubles and asked them to look for head trauma. I really didn't need to tell them to do this, but I was so frightened that she was still in danger.

As the staff attended to my daughter, I sat down and took a breath. Jill's helmet was still in my hands, a series of five deep gashes cut downward from the crown of the helmet, across the plexiglass face shield, and into the chin bar. I immediately recalled how we had, just that morning, decided that she should wear the full-face helmet instead of the ¾ version we more commonly took on long rides. Had she not been wearing the full-face helmet, she would have taken the rocks across her lovely face, and the damage would have been significant.

I don't recall how long the staff worked on Jill, but it was at least long enough for the Nevada Highway Patrol to arrive on the scene of the accident, call in a flatbed wrecker, and to bring our bikes to Caliente.

The damage to Jill ended up being minor. One broken bone, some road rash, and a mild concussion. They believed that the vision issue had come as a result of shock setting in.

I had called my wife shortly after arriving at the medical center, and she pulled up in my pickup truck a few hours later. We loaded the Intruder into the bed of my truck. The bike was a total loss, but it still rolled. Jillian rode home with Mom in the truck while I followed on the Harley.

Jill's accident had been a case of target fixation. She had been so concerned about not running off the road that she kept her eyes focused on the shoulder and, deep into a curve, the motorcycle took her there. "You go where you look" is a maxim of motorcycling, and Jill was still a bit green as a rider. I placed the fault on myself. I thought I was riding slow enough, and I had taught her well enough, but I should have been more cautious.

Though we were fortunate that my initial "worst fears" upon arriving at the accident scene were not realized, I have never really shaken the horrific dread that came over me when I faced the possibility of losing a child. This has affected how I feel when I now ride with my sons, Trent and Mitch. I am perhaps over-protective, and I tend to provide more advice and issue more warnings than they care to hear. I cannot help this. I also cannot help but worry that my passion for motorcycling–heck, that this entire Stephenson family obsession for motorcycling, (now in its third and fourth generations)– may lead to the death or serious injury to one of my treasured children or grandchildren.

After 19-year-old me had returned from a solo ride from Vegas to Seattle and back to Vegas, I remember my dad once telling me that, in his mind, he had tracked my every mile while I was gone, and his favorite sound was the exhaust note of my Beemer pulling back into the driveway. I didn't understand this until my own children began to ride.

I want to be clear–I still love motorcycling for all that it brings, but it also scares me to death for all that it can take away.

———

By 11:00 p.m., Trent and I were soaked and exhausted, so we found a motel in McComb, Mississippi, just a little shy of the Louisiana border. We'd covered 939 miles, even with the last half being in a monsoon. We'd started in Missouri and had added Illinois, Kentucky, Arkansas, Tennessee, and Mississippi to our total. The motel offered nothing for food, so I had to mount back up and head out to find an all-night drive through at a McDonalds. The food worker thought I was crazy on my motorcycle as we exchanged money for a sack of food in the driving rain.

CHAPTER 11
DAY FOUR
TUESDAY, MAY 30TH, 2017

It was still raining, but only lightly as we rolled out of McComb. Rain continued on-and-off for the entire morning on I-55, I-12, and I-10 through Louisiana and Alabama. Although I knew I couldn't spot it after all these years, and I doubted that it was even on this highway, I kept my eyes peeled on the side of the road in Alabama for an old-school motel to match a memory that had been aging for 48 years.

————

When I was ten years old, I took my first long-distance motorcycle ride when Dad put me on the buddy-seat behind him, and we rode his 1968 Harley FLH from Kansas City to Cape Canaveral, Florida. I remember but few snippets of the adventure. Like the time we rolled up behind a station wagon with its rear window down. As kids liked to do back in those days, two young brothers were laying down on their backs in the rear of the station wagon, and they had perched their bare feet out the rear window–kind of a defiant "thumbing of their noses" at the world behind them. As we passed the station wagon, Dad brought the sickle up tight to the left rear of the car and reached his right hand out in a feigned effort to grab these kids' feet. Their feet jerked back into the wagon as the boys shot bolt upright, eyes wide in fright at the prospect of being pulled out of the rear of the car at sixty miles an hour. Dad laughed. As we passed by the driver's window, the father of these two boys was having a good chuckle himself, and he gave us a friendly wave.

Certainly, my most vivid memory involved an incident at a motel that would become a story told and retold for decades to come in our family.

At dusk, after a long day of riding and probably somewhere in Alabama, Dad pulled the Hog into a roadside motel, the kind that was typical of small mom-and-pop lodgings in the '50s and '60s. There were perhaps thirty rooms, all at ground level, arranged in a squared-off horseshoe pattern with the parking lot in the center, a parking stall in front of each room. The office stretched across the opening of the horseshoe to partially close things off, and it featured an awning that served as the initial check-in spot for arriving motorists. I waited on the seat of the Harley while dad registered and obtained a key. Once checked in, dad wheeled the bike into the parking lot and backed it into the space in front of our room. We unloaded our gear and settled in as the last signs of light gave way to the night.

There's not much room for spare clothing in the saddlebags of a motorcycle, so we had no pajamas to change into. Dad stripped down to his skivvies as we got ready for bed. I had removed my shirt but still had on my blue jeans when I went into the bathroom to brush my teeth. Meanwhile, Dad searched through the pockets of his discarded pants for some loose change. He cracked open the front door to our room and peered outside. There was a pop machine on the sidewalk just outside of our room. Dad looked all around and saw only a couple of vacant parked cars, but no fellow travelers were outside of their rooms. Leaving the door to our room open, he chanced a quick dash in his underwear to the pop machine where he started feeding in nickels.

I came out of the bathroom and saw the front door open. I looked out the door, saw Dad at the pop machine, and joined him, closing the door behind me like I had always been told to do at home. I was, after all, a good boy and I didn't know that motel doors automatically lock behind you. Dad heard the click of the door, followed by my young voice, "Whatcha doin' Dad?"

Dad's hand remained frozen in place, poised to drop another nickel into the slot. His eyes shot first to the doorknob and then to me and then back to the doorknob. He jumped to the door and gave it a rattle. Nothing. His eyes shot around the parking lot, then he crouched to his knees behind the Harley as he pulled me close. His eyes were wide and incredulous, like he was searching my soul to determine whether I were really that empty-headed or if I were just that young. His words came quiet, with every syllable intently uttered: "Go to the front office. Ask for a second key. Do *not* tell the manager what has happened. Do *not* bring the manager back here with you. Just get another key. Understand?"

I nodded my head and scurried toward the office as a car came pulling into the parking lot, its headlight beams scanning across the motel rooms like the searchlights at a prisoner of war camp. Last I saw of Dad, he was stooped low behind the motorsickle and shuffling sideways in his underwear in an attempt to keep the bike between himself and the arriving travelers.

I obtained the second key without any questions, which is surprising now that I think about it, as I was a half-naked child asking for a motel room key. I guess that motel clerks have seen everything.

By the time I got back to the scene of my crime, which could not have been more than four minutes after I had left, Dad had somehow managed to get the door open and was inside the room. On the dresser, next to the TV was the motorcycle tool kit which we had left in the saddlebags when we had come in for the night. From that kit, he found means to pick the lock.

Even though I had caused Dad's embarrassment, and even though he was angry with me for a few moments, Dad still bought me a bottle of pop, but not until *after* he put his pants back on and took the key with him.

This family photo was taken around the time that the pop machine story took place. The Harley next to Dad is the same motorcycle we rode - the one he tried to hide behind in this story. I'm third from right, sitting on the Honda 50 I learned to ride on at eight years of age.

――――

Trent and I picked up a gas receipt in Pensacola, Florida, to complete our swing through the southernmost states. I noticed that the ground along the roads was composed less of soil and more of sand. The hibiscus flowers were in bloom and the palmettos were scattered in among the pines. Every time I visit Florida, my childhood home-state, I get a sense of melancholy brought on by being in familiar surroundings that remind me of the friends that are now missing in my life.

――――

After the Apollo space program was canceled in the early '70s, the Cape Canaveral area where I lived was, to a significant degree, vacated. Friends and neighbors pulled up stakes and chased jobs in other states. Our family's next adventure took us to Saudi Arabia, and I lost connection with most of those who were part of my Florida upbringing. The ghosts of those memories are felt every time I return to the Sunshine State, with some characters looming larger than others. Perhaps the largest was Forrest Fernaays.

It was the oddest friendship of my life. I figured he was fifty years older than I was. At fifteen years of age, I was a poor judge of the gray-haired crowd. I came to refer to him simply as "The Old Man," though I don't believe I ever called him that to his face. He cussed every time he saw me ride my Harley Sprint up to his shop on Hopkins Road in Titusville, Florida, but the Old Man, Forrest Fernaays, continues to play a pivotal role in my life nearly 45 years after our last conversation.

All that I knew of his past life was that he had spent time in the Navy before moving to Florida to open a motorcycle repair shop not far from where I lived. He was a touch under six feet tall, with a solid build earned by a life of hard work, and his gray hair was thick, though receding. Each arm featured faded tattoos (this was before all the chic people went for the ink), and he seemed to have a slight limp when he walked, but that may have been because he was so often crouched on a stool to wrench on a motor. The older I get, the better I understand the kinks that remain after arising from the floor.

He worked alone in his shop, which was filled primarily with older Harleys, Indians, and a British bike or two. When I rode up to his shop door after school, he usually shook his head and bellowed something like, "What the [bleep] do you want this time?" I usually just grinned back at his grumpiness, and he never actually chased me off with a mallet. Besides, there was always a wink behind the scowl, and each day, when I finally left, he would call out, "See you tomorrow, kid." Still, I sometimes brought Forrest a peace offering of a cold soda just to be sure he wouldn't get totally fed up with my hanging around.

One particular day, I was sitting on my usual old stool and doing most of the talking while Forrest wrenched on a motor. I carried on about my bright future–the big home I'd someday own and the long list of toys that would fill my garage–when I heard Forrest drop a wrench and firmly state my name. I quieted to see what he wanted.

With his back to me, while sitting on a bucket next to the motorcycle he was repairing, he shook his head. He turned and glanced at me, then looked back down at the floor in front of him. I remained silent as he let out a long breath before rising slowly to walk toward me. He craned his neck to see if there were any customers behind me, and I got the feeling he was either about to tell me a secret or he was finally going to knock me out. He certainly seemed interested in privacy at the time.

He drew close and spoke to me with an earnestness I hadn't heard before. He said, "Wes, you're an idiot. But that's okay because all kids your age are idiots."

I wondered, *was that the big secret or was this a preamble to a punch?*

Forrest continued, "You come in here and talk of all you are going to someday own and of all the people you are going to impress. But you don't even know who you are, and you sure don't know what really counts. Now, I'm going to share with you something I learned years ago – back when schools actually taught kids things, and I want you to listen closely."

Forrest again gave the door a glance to make sure we were alone, and he then presented me with the very last thing I could have expected from my burly friend. I stood dumbfounded as he recited from memory a poem.

When you get what you want in your struggle for wealth
And the world makes you king for a day;
Just go to the mirror and look at yourself
And see what that man has to say.

It isn't your father, your mother, or wife
Who judgment upon you must pass;
The fellow whose verdict counts most in your life
Is the guy staring back from the glass.

It's he you must please, never mind all the rest,
For he is with you clear up to the end;
You'll know that you've passed your most difficult test
When the man in the glass is your friend.

You may be like Jack Horner and chisel a plumb
And think you're a wonderful guy;
But the man in the glass says you're only a bum
If you can't look him straight in the eye.

You may fool the whole world down the pathway of years
And get a pat on the back as you pass;
But your final reward will be nothing but tears
If you've cheated the man in the glass.

THE MAN IN THE GLASS BY DALE
WIMBROW, CIRCA 1934

Forrest stopped. He looked back toward the door. He quietly added, "In the end, you need to be pleased with who you are, Wes. Just think about that." He bobbed his head once as if to add a period to his statement, then turned and headed back to work.

I was still blinking into space when Forrest sat down on his bucket and picked up his wrench.

I don't remember how I excused myself, but shortly after that repair shop recital, I was riding home, slowly motoring down the long route.

I don't know what amazed me most; that Forrest seemed to care that much about me or that a guy like that even knew a poem at all!

I thought about his message throughout the night and returned to Forrest's shop the next day with pencil and paper in hand. To my surprise, Forrest didn't seem annoyed as I asked him to recite each line of the poem as I scribbled it down. He again encouraged me to think about who it was I really wanted to be.

Not long after this, my father was transferred to Saudi Arabia, and our family followed. Forrest and I exchanged letters for a time, and he even admitted that he missed my pestering presence. While attending school in Arabia, I found an interest in poetry of "the manly nature"– poems like "The Cremation of Sam McGee" by Robert Service. Perhaps Forrest played a hand in showing me that poetry and masculinity can coexist as I developed a fondness for reading and writing poetry of the more traditional sort–an interest that I have followed to this day. By the time I graduated from high school and paid another visit to Titusville, Forrest's motorcycle shop was closed, and I could find no one who knew where he'd gone. I had no photos of my friend, but I'd kept one of his letters, and his image was burned into that portion of my mind reserved for mentors, idols, and exemplars.

Imagine my surprise when, not long ago, I did a Google search for his name and found a record on a genealogical website for Forrest G. Fernaays. I learned that he had lived to the age of 83 and was involved in motorcycling to the end. To my great delight, I found photos posted of my old friend taken in front of and inside his old shop in Titusville; the images are a perfect match of the vivid memories of my greasy guru.

———

Trent and I turned north on US-29 out of Florida to pick up I-65 in Alabama. Trent was feeling ill with a severe cold, and he was hoping to get a handle on it when we stopped to rest in Charlotte. In addition to the other leaks the Buell was experiencing, it became quite a challenge for Trent to deal with a runny nose, coughing, and sneezing while wearing a full-face helmet and while geared-up with gauntlet gloves. Every now and then he'd open his face shield to wash away any residue from his beard. Yuck.

We switched to I-85 near Montgomery and rode that highway all the way through Georgia, South Carolina, and into Charlotte. The interstate in South Carolina was under heavy construction and this slowed us significantly, often bringing us to a dead stop for extended periods. We were finally able to take off our rain suits which served as uncomfortable humidifiers; they not only kept rain out but also kept our bodies from breathing. Raingear also tends to flap in the wind, making my quiet BMW sometimes sound like my old Harley.

I always get a bit nervous when I wear loose riding gear on a motorcycle. This carries forward from an embarrassing experience I had in high school.

———

Toward the end of my sophomore year, my dad purchased a 1973 Honda 750 Four, and on occasion, he let me ride it to school. It was the largest displacement motorcycle on campus, and I was quite proud, to the point of being arrogant, that *my* bike was king of the hill.

One day after school, I climbed aboard the 750 and pulled out onto US-1 and rolled up directly behind the school bus that serviced the neighborhood where I lived. The bus was loaded with my friends, and a number of them gathered at the back window to wave and to make faces at me. Being "too cool for school," as they say, I ignored their antics and motored along with a detached, and probably imagined, "Fonzie Fonzarelli" air about me.

In the mid-'70s, bell bottom trousers were the rage, and I followed that fad. Unfortunately, and unbeknownst to me, as I rode along that day my right pant leg rose high on my calf from the 40-mph breeze. As the bus slowed to a stop at a traffic light, and as I likewise slowed, the pant leg lowered to slip down over my kickstart lever. When I came to a stop right behind the window full of my buddies, I was then unable to lower my leg as the bike leaned further and further to the right. To my horror, I could do nothing but stare into the stunned faces of my peers as I sat locked to the falling motorcycle until we were both parallel to the ground. The bus exploded with laughter as I crawled from underneath my motorcycle and initiated a few failed efforts to right the massive bike.

The bus was a block away before I finally got the 750 back on its wheels. I rode home and immediately made plans to convince my mom to let me call in sick for the rest of the school week. She would have none of it, and I had to face the teasing the very next day.

I learned that though motorcyclists tend to relish that "cool" image that comes with the territory, if the motorcyclist isn't careful, he may buy into that myth himself. Sooner or later, you learn that time will unmask you and reveal your foibles–so don't take yourself too seriously.

––––––

The construction delays in South Carolina were very frustrating to me, but Trent maintained his "whatever" nonchalance. At every stop ordered by a flag girl, I stewed over every minute we sat still, knowing it was another minute of sleep we would unavoidably miss since we had no choice but to ride on to Charlotte by the end of the day. We had appointments for motorcycle servicing early in the morning and those commitments couldn't be broken.

Over the headsets and on Bluetooth calls to the Harley shop and the Beemer shop throughout the day, we had planned each step of Wednesday's pit stop in Charlotte. If we could get the motorcycles serviced early in the morning, we might be able to make up at least a quarter or a half of a day by heading out earlier than we originally planned.

We arrived at my home in Charlotte at 2:30 in the morning under clear skies. We had put 837 miles and six more states under our belts that day, but we were still three-fourths of a day behind schedule, and I made clear to Trent my concerns that we may not be able to make up the time. He remained resolute that we *will* be able to do it, and his confidence, however unfounded, still encouraged me.

We also continued to get many words of encouragement from Facebook friends/followers from across the globe. Many told us that we were in their prayers. Some said they saw Heaven's hand in helping us get around and through the storms. I agreed though I would have preferred God us his almighty hand to withhold the rain.

CHAPTER 12
DAY FIVE
WEDNESDAY, MAY 31ST

I arose at 7:00, and Donna followed me in the van as I rode the Beemer to South Charlotte to drop it off for tires and an oil change when the dealer opened at 8:00. I told them about the instability issues, and they said they'd look into it. They were well aware of my Iron Butt Challenge, and they double-teamed the work, but it would still be at least three hours before completed. Donna and I headed back home, but not before stopping to purchase a new battery for the Buell. We hadn't had any more trouble starting the bike since that rainy day in Mississippi, but I wasn't happy with how quickly that battery had lost power. The Harley dealer in Statesville (quite a ways north of Charlotte) still had not received the fork seals and brake pads for the Buell, but the shipping tracker showed that the parts would arrive that morning. So, when Donna and I got home, I pulled the windshield off the Buell and Trent headed out on the bike for the Harley shop with Donna following him in her van. The plan was for them to drop the Buell off in Statesville, return to our house to get me and my gear, and the three of us would drive down to get the BMW sometime before noon. With Donna and Trent in the van and me once again astride the Beemer, we would then head north for Statesville where the Buell should be fixed by the early afternoon, and Trent and I would leave from there.

"Best laid plans...."

While they were gone, I sat about working in the garage.

Now, I know that motorcycles are inanimate, lacking the capacity for independent thought, but I couldn't help but feel guilty as I worked next to Big Red. I somehow sensed (or imagined) the Harley's resentment at having been left behind on this adventure. It really was a very capable motorcycle even if it lacked all the features that had come along in the 27 years since it rolled off the assembly line. And it was lightyears ahead of the Harleys Dad had long ago taken across the continent, and it was miles beyond the first Harley big twin I had ridden.

First of all, let's define "big motorcycles" as understood in the early 1970s because, in those days, that tag held a different connotation than it does today. Through the '50s and '60s there were two classes of "big bikes." Harley's version and everybody else's. To the Brits and Europeans, engine displacement up until the '70s seemed to be capped in the 650-750cc range. The biggest BSA's, Triumph's, and Royal Enfield's were 650cc twins. Germany's BMW R60 and R69S models, considered by many to be the most reliable long-distance motorcycles on the market, pushed riders across continents with only 600cc engines, while Italy's largest offering was Moto Guzzi's 750cc Ambassador. These were all very capable motorcycles that transported countless riders across vast distances, as I can attest, having ridden my 600cc 1966 BMW across the United States several times.

In America, the country's only remaining motorcycle manufacturer, Harley Davidson, had long lived in the world of big-displacement motors, the best-known of which was their 74-cubic-inch (1200cc) big twin that powered their "King of the Highway" Electra Glide.

———

During Christmas break 1975, I flew from my boarding school in the country of Bahrain to visit my parents in Jeddah, Saudi Arabia. While there, my dad took me to visit one of his coworkers, who owned a 1969 Harley Electra Glide. During the visit, the man offered to let me take the big twin for a ride. I was nervous, but inwardly, I was wagging my little motorcycle-doggie-tail at the thought of finally operating the legendary Harley 74, the motorcycle that had been central to so many of the stories my dad had shared throughout my childhood. This behemoth was far larger in displacement than the biggest bike I'd ridden to that point (my dad's Honda 750), and each of its twin cylinders exploded with the combined volume of the two combustion chambers of my 600cc BMW.

I drew a deep breath and swung a leg over the tall saddle, suspended above the frame of the bike on a pivot dampened by a hydraulic seat post. Dad had sold his own Electra Glide a few years prior, and after a childhood spent climbing up onto dad's Harleys in our garage and playing make-believe with my legs splayed straight out and my hands unable to reach both grips at the same time, this was the first time I'd straddled a big Hog and had been able to plant both feet on the ground while resting my hands comfortably on the controls. The grips were meaty and filled my fists; I felt as if I were shaking the calloused hands of a stone worker. I tested the tension on the brake and clutch levers and found that their reputation for stiff pulls was well-deserved. Dad had always told me that the hand levers of a Harley were like some sort of Charles Atlas apparatus, designed to build the muscles in the forearms.

Dad and his buddy walked me through the controls: starter button, rear brake, front brake, clutch, shift lever. All of which were generally located in the same positions as they were on the bikes to which I was accustomed. It wasn't their positions that seemed foreign to me, it was their exaggerated operations that felt alien. As already mentioned, the pull effort at the hand controls was at least twice that of the bikes I had ridden. The rear brake pedal on nearly all other motorcycles is situated just in front of the right footpeg and below the ball of the foot. A simple rocking downward of the foot engages the rear brake on most motorcycles. On the Harley, the rear brake is an enormous rectangular pedal that seems to be straight out of the floorboard of a 1938 Buick. It is situated at the front of a footboard (not a footpeg) that fully supports the soles of the boot. To engage the brake, the entire right leg is involved as the thigh rises to lift the foot, the lower leg swings forward to kick the foot into the pedal, and the rider's entire right limb is tensioned to depress the pedal.

On the left side of most motorcycles, the gear shift lever is situated in a nearly identical position in front of the footpeg as is the brake lever on the right side of the bike. Small downward or upward movements of the left foot ratchets the lever from one gear to another in a series of clicks. However, on the Harley, a hefty rocker bar sits above the footboard, just to the side of the lower engine casing. A thumb-sized peg protrudes from each end of the rocker bar and, to change gears, the left foot is lifted to either stomp down on the front peg to downshift or to similarly come down on the rear peg to upshift.

All these differences flooded my mind as I sat in the saddle and prepped myself for that first ride. The large movements and long throws would become even more pronounced once underway, but I could already sense that riding this motorcycle would be more akin to managing a locomotive than operating my familiar BMW.

I flipped on the ignition switch, which was mounted near the gauges in the center of the fuel tank. I depressed a round black button on the right handlebar, and the big twin came to life as the entire motorcycle shuddered below me and trembled in my hands. The massive motor was bolted solid into the frame with no rubber mounts, causing every blast from the staggered power strokes to contribute to the shaking. Still, it wasn't an annoying vibration like the high frequency, low amplitude buzz of some bikes I'd ridden. There was satisfaction in the syncopation that resonated in my bones and blended into my being. The tremors hit you as a surprise, at first, when your previous mounts have not produced these peculiar impulses, but it declares a vitality that is undeniable.

I drew in the clutch lever, raised my left boot from the ground and dropped it down on the front peg of the shifter. The resulting CLUNK was loud and satisfying, like the sound of train car couplers snapping shut to grasp another freight car in a death grip. A quick shiver, coming from deep within the transmission suggested that the gears were engaged and ready to be released. Nervous that I would stall the motor in front of my dad and his friend, I rolled the throttle on heavier than I needed to and attempted to feather out the clutch. The powerful clutch springs overruled my intentions, and the lever lurched out of my grasp. The Harley launched forward, jerking my head back as it pounced. Feet up, I was on my way.

The Harley handlebars were wide and gave the feel that this ship had a solid tiller–she went where you pointed her until you pointed her elsewhere. From my BMW, I was accustomed to shifting before the RPMs climbed too high, and I initiated the choreography previously described for changing gears. I hauled in the clutch as I eased on the throttle, stomped on the rear rocker peg, and let loose the clutch lever. The Hog accepted my initiatives without complaint, and as I rolled on the throttle in second gear, the handlebars and seat pulsed forward to draw me into the oncoming air, the tractor-like torque hard-wired to that right hand grip. I completed two more shifts to reach the top of four gears and enjoyed the deepened voice that barked from the fishtail pipes when the motor strained against the load of acceleration. At cruising speed, the exhaust notes seemed to come only once every thirty feet.

Bringing the Harley to a halt was much more physical than I had expected. My left hand flexed repeatedly against strong clutch tension; my left knee bounced up and down as the arch of my boot ratcheted down on the rocker peg in a series of downshifts, while my right-side appendages dealt with that Buick brake pedal down low and with the high-resistance effort of the front brake lever on the right handlebar.

The ride was not particularly long, only a mile or two in one direction before turning around to bring the Hog back to its barn. At the end of the ride, I was relieved to have completed the exercise without stalling the engine or dropping the bike.

On the drive home, Dad asked me what I thought of my first ride in command of a full-fledged "74." A few thoughts came to mind, including "Massey-Ferguson" and "Farmall." The adjectives that followed included, intentional, solid, engaged, beefy, and soulful. The power was not delivered with the acceleration of a slingshot but with the steady *it-won't-be-stopped* determination of a hydraulic press—it just kept coming, unaffected by hill or headwind.

It would be five more years before I would again ride a Harley big twin. In 1980, at age twenty-two, I purchased my first new Harley Davidson. It was an 80 cubic inch black Electra Glide; its 1340cc shovelhead engine was the largest displacement motorcycle available at that time. The many advancements made by Harley since that '69 model made it an easier ride (better brakes, smoother controls), but the motorcycle still retained the feature that had stuck with me for five long years—the years when I had saved up my pennies and squirreled away my dimes to once again experience this central element—the big twin that beats with the heart of a locomotive. I've now owned many models of Harleys over the years, and quite a few of those were newer than Big Red, but this bike somehow remained my "main squeeze," even if I cheated on her now and again.

———

I turned my back on Big Red and continued my chores. I had an extra windshield from my Harley (old and a little discolored, but for some reason, I'd never tossed it out). I pulled it down from the garage rafters and trimmed it down and drilled holes to match up with the hardware from the Buell's windshield. While it would not end up as large as it was when it mounted on my full-dress Hog, it ended up being quite a bit larger than the pitiful unit that came stock on the Buell. My hope was to give the Buell rider a better "protection bubble" from the elements, but I was concerned that the light-gauge mounting hardware from the small windshield might not hold up against this larger shield.

————

This wasn't my first experience fashioning a makeshift windshield in the middle of a ride. My mind drifted back to that father-son trip of 1974 when, somewhere in Montana, I had once again dropped my motorcycle in a parking lot. But this time, the windshield cracked in half vertically. Dad obtained a piece of plexiglass at a hardware store and cut it down to shape using my broken windshield as a pattern. The windshield worked okay; the only trouble being that once we hit 70 miles per hour, the top of the windshield bent back toward me. This meant that, at highway speeds, I had to ride with one hand propping up the windshield. Once we hit Kansas City, where my grandparents lived, Dad made another windshield from sturdier stock.

Around 10:00, I got a call from the Harley shop telling me that the parts we were waiting for had arrived at another Harley dealer many states away, and it would be another day before we could get them brought to Statesville. *Of course,* I thought as I could no longer fight off the discouragement. *If anything can go wrong, it will.*

Trent and Donna had already dropped the Buell off at the shop, and so I had to call to inform them that they needed to turn around and retrieve the Buell and bring it back home. Once they returned, Trent and I installed the windshield (which didn't look too bad by-the-way) and we installed the new battery. I took off the front brake calipers and cleaned the pads with brake cleaner and scuffed them on my belt-sander. The fork fluid wasn't leaking as bad now that most of the fluid was apparently gone (not ideal but not critical either). The BMW shop called to say my bike was ready, though they found no issues that would lead to instability, and they said their test-ride felt normal.

We picked up the BMW a little after noon, and with fresh food and clean laundry packed in our saddlebags, we headed north on I-77. Trent reported that the "custom" windshield was a real improvement, and that the brackets held up well against high-speed winds, despite pushing the larger shield. The brakes, too, were far improved after the cleaning. As for the stability issues on the Beemer, the tires didn't fix the matter. It was not at all a safety concern, just a nit-pick item that annoyed me over time–always having to give the bars a little corrective pressure, one side or the other, to keep the nose pointed at the target. My mind drifted back to one of my earliest lessons on motorcycle control.

———

On a warm spring evening in 1974, Dad popped open the door to my bedroom, "Hey Wes, how about we ride the 'Hondoo' down to Cocoa Beach for a milkshake?"

I'd jumped to my feet before he'd even finished the question. Dad had just bought his Honda 750-Four, and I hadn't yet had the chance to take a ride on it. I slipped on my gray leather jacket and followed Dad to the clapboard single-car garage that stood behind our home in Titusville, Florida. In the dark, the Harley 350 Sprint that was my usual ride to high school lurked, and next to that, Dad's four-cylinder Honda stood. Dad backed the Honda out onto the drive, fired it up, and signaled me to climb onto the back seat.

We rode south on US-1, took the A1A east across the Indian River, then over the Banana River to turn south again on Cape Canaveral. The ocean breeze smelled sweet, and the two-lane coastal highway was flanked on both sides by stately two-story frame homes wrapped in large screened-in verandas that encircled both levels. The bike was velvet, yet when Dad gave the right grip a twist, the machine shot forward at a rate I'd never experienced. What a thrill.

We didn't spend much time at the burger joint where we downed a couple of root beer freezes, and as we walked back to where the Honda was parked, Dad asked me, "Would you like to take the controls?"

At 15, I'd never operated a bike bigger than my 350, and this Honda was more than twice that size, and it produced three times the horsepower. I gulped, smiled, and settled into the front seat. Dad mounted up behind me and gave me a few instructions. I lit the four cylinders and noticed that just a slight blip of the throttle shot the RPM's up in a hurry. My effort to get her rolling was less than smooth, but we were soon northbound on A1A.

I was careful not to wrap up the engine, as I could feel I was bumping into some serious acceleration every time the tach rose above

3500 rpm, so I short-shifted probably more than I should have. The bike was stable and, again, incredibly smooth. I followed the luminated tunnel of light created by the Honda's headlamp as it bored through the overhanging trees.

A short while into the ride, Dad put a hand on my shoulder and commented, "You're doing a fine job, son."

I turned my head to the side to comment back, "Thanks, Dad. This is really-"

"LOOK OUT!" My Dad shouted.

I spun my head back around and saw a large yellow sign with black arrows pointing to the left, warning drivers that the road no longer continued in the northerly direction and that the change would be abrupt. Before I could react, Dad pushed forward on my left elbow, and the motorcycle immediately dove hard to the left and into the curve. In two blinks of an eye, we were through the corner, and Dad pushed forward on my right elbow this time and the bike righted itself. We were again centered up on the road.

I heard Dad mutter, "I may have spoken too soon," as my heart settled down from the fright.

We rode the rest of the way home a bit slower than normal, but without any other incidents. After putting the bike away, I had to ask Dad to explain something to me.

"When I was about to overshoot that left-hand turn, you pushed forward on my left arm which pressured the handlebars to the right. That should have sent us off the road to the right. How did it end up that we turned to the left?"

Dad bobbed his head once or twice and explained, "Whether you realize it or not, that's how you commonly steer your motorcycle, or even your bicycle for that matter. You push the bars to the right to turn left, and vice-versa. It's called *counter-steering,* and everyone who can ride a two-wheeler does this as a learned habit, usually without even being conscious of their actions."

"No way", I responded, "I would know if I was turning the bars the opposite direction in making a turn."

"Apparently, son–you are among those who can ride a bike despite not really knowing how you do it. Once you are underway, and at anything above walking speed on a two-wheeler, you actually and routinely initiate your turns by pressing your handlebars away from the direction you want to go. Some claim it has something to do with the gyroscopic effect of the spinning tire and wheel assembly, creating a counter force to the rider's input. Others say that the bar pressures simply cause the front wheel to drive out from under the rider to the right, for example, which initiates a lean to left. The leaning wheels then work like a pair of pizza cutters to climb into the curve to the left. Whatever the reason, the harder you push in one direction, the deeper the bike dives the other way into the turn."

Dad could tell I was still skeptical, even though his quick reactions on the motorcycle twenty minutes earlier had clearly demonstrated the truth of what he was telling me. "Just try it next time you ride the Sprint, or even your bicycle. Get up to speed and take your hands off the bars. Then push forward on one side or the other and see which way you turn."

I followed his suggestion the next day and was amazed that I'd never before realized how my bike actually steers.

In the years since, I have read countless articles in motorcycle magazines, and I've listened to podcasts from motorcycle experts teaching the "art of counter-steering," as if it was a newly discovered thing or a special technique that only the best riders can utilize. In reality, this skill is already a part of every rider once the training wheels came off their first Schwinn, even if they are unaware of how they do what they do.

In the intervening years, I have often thought about the lesson learned by my dad's push of my elbow toward a direction that was opposite to what logic might dictate. I have come to see that this counterintuitive principle is repeated as a pattern in so many facets of life. Two examples: whether or not it makes sense at the outset, we are more enriched by what we give than by what we are given. There is greater peace and satisfaction in forgiving others than in retribution or revenge. There are just so many times in life when the right way to turn seems to be opposite of the first instinct. This insight is yet another valued waypoint that I have been brought to by virtue of "the ride."

————

Trent and I entered Virginia, taking gas in Hillsville, then Wyers Cave, and finally stopped for the night at Woodstock. There was a very precocious young girl, about six years old, in the lobby of the motel with whom we had a bit of fun. Wide eyed, she asked us questions and seemed to think we were something out of the movies with our leather chaps, jackets, and bandannas. Her family asked if we would pose for pictures with their sweet daughter.

Three hundred twenty-five miles were covered on this, our shortest day of riding. We were now halfway through our time allotment but not yet halfway through the needed distance. We really needed the next day to be a 1000-mile day in order to get ourselves back in position to complete the entire circuit in ten days.

CHAPTER 13
DAY SIX

THURSDAY, JUNE 1ST

Trent and I got a good, early start before the rising sun, and took gas at 7:40 a.m. in Harper's Ferry, West Virginia. We were enthralled by the gorgeous countryside in this Blue Ridge region, and we took turns pointing out scenic farmlands, quaint buildings, and historic markers along the way. We picked up our Maryland gas receipt in White Marsh and our Delaware receipt in Newark. We were pleased, and frankly surprised to be avoiding heavy traffic fairly well as we rolled through Philadelphia on I-95. We had been concerned that this densely populated portion of the country would really eat into our cruising speeds, and so we were thrilled to be making up precious time and miles. As we rode, I thought about that little girl from the hotel lobby the previous night and her request to have her picture taken with us. I saw in her eyes a wonder toward motorcycles and their riders that I recognized from my own childhood.

There's an old Willie Nelson song that declares, "My Heroes Have Always Been Cowboys," and for Willie and for many of my childhood playmates, it was the western hero that filled their sights. For me, it was motorcycle riders, but for the very same reasons that my buddies idolized cowboys. I had grown up imagining the characters that were central to my father's tales of motorcycle adventures from his youth, and I'd come to know a few of those who had remained close to Dad as years rolled on. I admired their adventurous spirits, their resourcefulness, and their *code of the road* that mirrored the old *code of the west*. I devoured every monthly edition of *Harley's Enthusiast* magazine and followed the racing careers of Dick Mann, Cal Rayborn, Mert Lawwill, and a young Jay Springsteen. As an 11-year-old, I tuned in every Wednesday night to watch Michael Parks ride his Sportster across America in the TV show *Then Came Bronson,* and I read every news article that tracked the adventures of the daredevil, Evel Knievel, (I would later sponsor Evel's son, Robbie, through my tire stores in Las Vegas).

Eventually, a story didn't even need to focus on motorcycles–it only needed to be somehow associated with a motorcycle–to rivet my attention and lock a story or event into my memory banks. I guess that's how it works for many of us who are obsessed with a hobby, a team, or a topic–we become trivia savants who forget nothing that has the slightest connection with our chosen interest.

––––––

The following story is not really about the motorcycle, though I'm sure that the fact that a motorcycle is part of the story helped capture my attention at the time and then cemented the memory into my mind. It is the tale of the most horrific motorcycle ride I've ever heard of or, for that matter, that I could even imagine.

After my freshman year of college, I took a break from motorcycles, girls, and most other pursuits as I served a two-year mission for my church. I was excited to be assigned to labor in South Africa. After two months of intense language training to learn Afrikaans (lovingly referred to as "Dutch with marbles in your mouth"), I arrived in Johannesburg in November of 1977. I was immediately shipped out to the town of Potchefstroom on the Transvaal where few spoke English as their first language.

A month or two into our efforts there, my partner and I knocked on a cottage door and were surprised to be greeted in English by an Anglo man with charcoal-gray hair and a deeply lined face. I guessed him to be in his mid-to-late fifties. After a quick exchange of greetings, he surmised, "You blokes are Yanks, aren't you?"

My companion confirmed the man's assessment as I tried to train my ear on the man's accent. He wasn't South African, but I couldn't be sure if he was Kiwi, Aussie, or from somewhere in the British Isles. He solved the riddle before I could ask, "I'm from Brighton, UK"

He invited us inside where we were introduced to his wife and to his son, a tall, lean, and shaggy-haired young man in his mid twenties. We spent a while getting acquainted. They didn't run across many Americans, and they seemed to enjoy our accents as much as we did theirs. We learned that both the old man and his son worked at the gold mines outside of town.

We soon got to our reason for knocking on their door that evening as we shared with them a message about a god who could be active in our lives, one who cares for His children and has provided a compassionate plan for our peace and for finding true joy. The discussion went well, and we closed with a prayer before bidding the family farewell.

As we stepped onto the porch, the old man followed us and closed the door behind him. He accompanied us along the walkway to where we had chained our bicycles to a streetlamp near the curb. In the yellow halo of the lamplight, he stood staring at the ground for a moment before clearing his throat, "Boys, I want to tell you a story if you have a few more minutes."

We nodded to encourage him to go on.

His voice was low, and his eyes remained downcast, "At the outbreak of World War II, I did as all the lads did, and I signed up to fight the Nazis. I was assigned to the Royal Corps of Signals and trained as a motorcycle messenger."

He paused, and I leaned in to hear better. He raised his head to look me in the eyes, "Radio transmission was not only spotty back then, but they were easy for the enemy to intercept. We were trained to ride our motorcycles in, around, and through all kinds of terrain and obstacles to deliver important communication between commanders."

He took a deep breath before continuing, "We were thick in the middle of things in Italy when two of my fellows and I were called to a field office. We were told of a company of Yankee GIs who were surrounded by the Germans in a stand of woods a few miles away. There was a plan for breaking them free, but they needed to know the timing and the nature of the allied counterattack. Those plans were shared verbally with the three of us dispatch riders."

The old man looked off into the distance, "We knew why they had chosen three of us to deliver the message instead of just one. Redundancy. We were to ride like bats out of hell through the German lines to reach the Yanks, and though no one said it out loud, we knew there was a less-than-even chance of any one of us getting through alive.

"We rode off late in the afternoon, and I'm certain that I was shaking more than my motorbike. One of my mates seemed awfully anxious to get to the German lines because he quickly shot out far ahead of me and the other rider. It then dawned on me that the lead man would have the advantage over the other two riders as he would be past the unsuspecting Germans before they could even raise their rifles to shoot. The following riders would surely not be as fortunate. My buddy and I flogged our BSA's in an effort to catch up to the lead rider."

I looked over at my missionary partner, but his eyes remain fixed on the old man, who had paused only briefly,

"The Jerrys had a nasty habit of stringing piano wire between trees along the paths through the woods, a booby trap for any enemy coming along on motorbikes or in Jeeps. The fellow on the lead bike hit a wire and was killed instantly; his head nearly severed from his body. Seeing this, we then left the trail and picked our way through the woods. We soon heard excited shouts coming from God-knows-where within the forest, and this was followed soon enough by the rapport of rifles. I never actually saw the enemy—only heard the shots and saw bark explode from the trees around me as I rode full-throttle through the forest."

He swallowed once, then twice, and his lips pursed to control his emotions. "We soon emerged from the trees and entered an enormous pasture, flat and smooth, and probably five hundred yards across. Another wall of trees awaited us on the far side of the field, and I assumed it was there that the Yanks were to be found.

"My buddy was riding twenty yards in front of me, and I fell in behind his track. The bullets kept coming but were quickly joined by shells exploding all around us."

The old man's eyes glistened solemnly, and I felt my own begin to well, empathizing with the horror this boyish rider must have felt.

The old man continued, "I've never been so afraid in my life. The tears streamed straight back on my face as I wept, keeping my focus on my buddy's muddy back and the tree line in front of us. It was then that the motorcycle in front of me exploded into a cloud of mud, blood, and bolts..." The old man's jaw jutted out as he determinedly uttered the next description, "...and I rode through that cloud, pelted by all that had disintegrated before me, hanging loosely onto my bike as it bounced and bucked over the final fifty yards to the pines.

"I crashed the bike into a barrier made of logs, and I tumbled to a stop among the ferns. An enormous pair of hands grabbed me by the shoulders and dragged me deeper into the woods and down into a ditch already occupied by a half-dozen GIs. I laid there, shaking, and trying to stop my sobs when a Yankee sergeant knelt next to me, handed me a flask of whisky, and said, 'Here—you're going to need this.'"

The old man then let out another deep breath then raised his eyes to mine, "I had never touched hard liquor before in my life. But from that day to this, the bottle has never left my side." He bowed his head and slowly shook it side to side, "And that has been the tragedy of my life."

I looked at my companion—his wide eyes and open mouth likely a mirror of my own. The old man lifted his head again, "And I want better for my son. I want him to have something better to turn to than the numbness that comes from the bottle. I want you to come back and teach him about this *better path* you spoke about. Will you do that for me?"

My partner and I remained stunned. We were shell shocked by his story and could not fathom the soul-shaking experience that this man had lived through. We could not even begin to judge poorly of this man for the path his life took—no—we admired him for his hard-earned wisdom and for the fatherly love he obviously felt for his son. We promised to return the next night to share with him and his family a far better way.

He seemed satisfied with that as he simply turned and walked back up the path toward his house.

Neither my partner nor I uttered a word as we mounted our bicycles and pedaled down the lane. I could almost smell gunpowder and feel the shudder of mortar shells as we rode toward our boarding house. The thought then came to me that I had just been delivered a very costly and most significant message—a message 35 years in transit and delivered that night in an obscure South African village by a brave and honorable dispatch rider from Britain's Royal Corps of Signals.

———

By the time Trent and I hit Pennsylvania, I was riding the Buell. We were in moderate traffic just north of Philly, and I-95 was four lanes in this section. I was following a van pulling a flatbed trailer and waiting for an opening on my right to pass the slower vehicle. When the opening came, I shifted lanes to the right. Just as I was about to cross the centerline, I caught a flashing glimpse of an enormous chuckhole as it emerged from hiding under the flatbed trailer. Both of the motorcycle's wheels hit hard on the sharp far edge of this asphalt abyss, and both the front and rear shocks bottomed-out from the impact, sending a jolt up my spine that, I swear, ricocheted around my helmet to run back down my backbone and launch my butt high into the air. I nearly lost hold of the handlebars from the impact, but the bike remained stable.

I was sure this must have blown the rear tire, but I didn't sense any swaying or tell-tale signs of a flat. I keyed my mic and asked Trent to swing in behind me and tell me if my tire was going flat. He pulled in behind, and a few seconds later, he told me to get off the road; the tire was going down fast.

There was a fast-approaching exit, and I made my way to it. I was not even able to ride up to the intersection as the tire lost all air, and I came to a stop next to the guardrail halfway up the exit ramp. Trent pulled in behind me. We inspected the tire to see if there was a hole that we could plug (I brought a plug kit on the trip for this purpose). Unfortunately, in addition to a hole in the tire, the wheel itself was bent so that the tire could not be seated to hold air even if we patched the hole. We did not have the tools/equipment to remove the wheel or for me to attempt to straighten the wheel (as I have done scores of times during my career in the tire industry).

Trent called a tow company, and they indicated that they would arrive with a flatbed within 40 minutes. For me, these 40 minutes were interminably long as I sat on the guardrail, my mind searching for solutions but arriving at none. This injury to the Buell would take many hours to rectify and would probably cost us more time than we could make up in the days remaining on the clock. Trent was not at all distraught as he seemed to personify our originally stated creed for this ride: safety was first priority; completing the circuit was our second objective; completing the circuit within ten days would be a real coup, but it was still last on the list. I could repeat the creed, but I just couldn't feel it.

The tow truck arrived, and Trent rode the bike onto the ramp of the flatbed where they secured it with straps. Trent clowned around to lighten the mood and suggested that the driver take us the rest of the way to Utah with Trent riding the Buell from the bed of the truck.

The driver was friendly and took us to a nearby Harley dealership, Brian's Harley Davidson in Langhorne, PA. We explained to the service writer and parts manager the urgent nature of our ride. They were aware of the 48 State challenge, but they had never known anyone to have actually done it. They were also appreciative of the veterans' cause we were supporting, and they got the bike in as quickly as possible. They pulled the wheel and intended to have a local wheel repair shop do the repair. Unfortunately, the wheels on this Buell were not made of aluminum as is most common on bikes and cars, but they were instead crafted of magnesium, and no one was comfortable in straightening the bend for fear of cracking it. Even if it *appeared* to be fine after the repair, a crack could still manifest later, and a failed wheel could cause a blowout at highway speeds, particularly the speeds we would need to make up time. We decided that we could not take that chance–the 48 State certificate was not worth a life. The only replacement wheel was at the factory in Milwaukee, and they could overnight it to us. We ordered the wheel.

At that moment, I felt like Apollo 13 astronaut Jim Lovell, when, in the midst of chaotic efforts to salvage the mission after one problem followed another, he was ordered to turn off a valve that could not be turned back on, and that action spelled the certain end of his target goal of landing on the moon. I actually turned to Trent in the service bay and said, "We just lost the moon." It was no longer humanly possible to complete our ride in the prescribed time frame. The rules do not provide exceptions for weather nor for mechanical failures. You either complete the ride in 240 hours, or you do not.

We stashed our excess luggage into the service manager's office so that we could ride two-up on the Beemer. Trent and I rode to a Red Roof Inn and checked into our room to assess what we would do next. Still smacking from realizing that we had just "lost the moon," for some reason my mind turned to, of all things, women's tennis.

The *Grand Slam* of tennis is the elusive honor of winning the title in all four major tournaments during a single calendar year, and it's a very rare feat. In 2002, Serena Williams won the final three major tournaments of that year, and then, in 2003, she won the first major tournament to complete what would come to be known as the "Sarena Slam." She was still the reigning champion of all four events, but they had not technically been won in the same calendar year, so this was not recognized as a true Grand Slam.

I knew that the Iron Butt Association recognition was no longer possible. We would not be earning their certificate. But we could still complete our own version of the Sarena Slam. Our new goal was to complete the ride in ten days of actual RIDING (disregarding mechanical downtime) even if the Iron Butt Association would not recognize this ride. *We* would still know that we had demonstrated the physical stamina and drive to accomplish the feat. As Rocky would say, "I can't win; I just want to go the distance." All that was left was for us to prove to ourselves that, barring incidents out of our control, we could do this.

We took a long walk to a Red Robin for a full sit-down dinner and then got a good, long night's rest for the first time since the start of the adventure.

CHAPTER 14
DAY SEVEN
FRIDAY, JUNE 2ND, 2017

In the morning, I posted to our Facebook followers the sad news of the broken wheel and let them know that the ten-day window was now lost—that goal could no longer be accomplished. I thanked them for their support:

"While I have a few unexpected hours available in the midst of this journey, I want to thank those who have already made this effort an enormous success: Trent and I had an ambitious goal of raising $2000 for The Independence Fund (providing all-terrain wheelchairs to disabled veterans) through a Go Fund Me account. Thanks to all of you, we have already blown through this goal and have provided an incredible $2430 for these most-deserving heroes. Donations have come from strangers and from brand-new friends; from longtime friends (even childhood friends I have not seen in decades); from coworkers and Tire Pros dealers across the country who already do so much for this noble cause; and from my wonderful and supportive family. This world needs more hearts like yours, and Trent and I thank you for being a part of our team."

I shared with them our revised goal of completing the circuit in ten "riding days," and the responses we received were overwhelmingly supportive.

We had hoped for a late-morning arrival of the wheel, but this proved to be "the watched pot that never boils." We hung around the Harley shop all morning and spoke with a number of riders who came through, and our crazy 48-state ride seemed to be of interest to them all.

At one point, I was checking again with the parts manager to see if he'd heard anything from FedEx tracking, when a customer told me about the time that he "almost" made the trip to the Sturgis motorcycle rally in South Dakota. He lamented that he had the ride all lined up, he had saved up the money, and had arranged for the time off. He was going to ride out there with another guy who ended up backing out, and so he didn't go. He said, "Too bad; I'll probably never have the chance to do that again."

His statement really ticked me off. Why do people pine away for things they are unwilling to chase–things that *could* be theirs if they only decided to go grab it? Missing out on his Sturgis dream is not the fault of his friend who backed out on him. This "miss" rested squarely on his own shoulders.

So, I went into my calendar speech. I simply asked him if he owned a calendar. He looked puzzled but replied, "Yes." I then informed him that he could go to Sturgis if he owned a calendar, and I then went on to explain that the primary reason that people don't do things like this is that they don't mark a date and make a declaration that they are going to go do it. I challenged him to take out a marker, circle a date, even if it was three years out, and then tell his whole world that, by gum, he's going to Sturgis.

Unfortunately, the man just stared at me, giving no indication that he understood the power of making a commitment to take action. I felt certain that he was doomed to only read about Sturgis in magazines, simply for the lack of a circled date on a two-dollar calendar.

The wheel did not arrive until after lunch, but the mechanic jumped right on it and the job was done in thirty minutes. After a day and a half delay, we reloaded the Buell with Trent's gear and headed back out on I-95–watching more carefully for Pennsylvania potholes!

We passed through New Jersey and crossed the George Washington Bridge into New York, eventually catching I-91 in Connecticut heading for Hartford. We called ahead to my daughter, Jillian, who lives in Harford, and we arranged to meet her, her husband, Ben, and their four kids at an exit off I-84. We made the rendezvous, and after a nice but brief visit and a sit-down dinner, we continued east before stopping for the night at Dover, Connecticut, just shy of the Rhode Island border.

We were glad to be back in the race now. Our new goal was to hit the 48th state, Utah in our case, by 6:00 a.m. on Thursday, June 8th to complete our version of the "Stephenson Slam" of the 48 states in ten days of riding. We were in New England and the day ahead would collect states quickly, where the states were the size of our counties out west.

CHAPTER 15
DAY EIGHT
SATURDAY, JUNE 3RD, 2017

Trent and I rode on some nice country roads into the northwestern corner of Rhode Island (there were no major highways here), and the travel was picturesque even if it was slow. We gassed in Chepachet, then turned north for Massachusetts where we caught the turnpike toward Boston. We avoided Beantown by taking the 495 north to I-95 near the New Hampshire border, then rode the coast through New Hampshire to Kittery, Maine–the easternmost point in our journey.

There are no major east-west highways across New Hampshire or Vermont, so we took Hwy 4 and 9 through those two states. This was unavoidably slow, winding as it did through one small New England town after another, but it was beautiful, and we enjoyed this as much as our impatience would allow. This stretch allowed us to *play* with our motorcycles in the curves in a way that none of our interstate roads had allowed us to do thus far. For those of you inexperienced in motorcycle riding, let me share some aspects of the sport that you may not be aware of (be patient as I explain this one).

We pulled off the highway to take a photo by a lobster sign and to briefly celebrate the apex of our circuit.

Growing up as I did at Cape Canaveral, Florida, in the height of the Space Race, it seemed that every dad, and many of the moms, were somehow engaged in the effort to launch things into orbit, and I learned that things in orbit are perpetually "falling" toward the gravitational pull of the planet or moon around which they are circling. The satellite or spacecraft only misses crashing into the planet or moon by virtue of the velocity they maintain and the "centrifugal force" (for lack of the engineer's term) that this creates. A higher velocity moves the satellite or spacecraft into a wider orbit, and a slower velocity moves the craft into a tighter orbit.

Think about the penny you may have dropped into one of those vortex funnels at the arcade. At first, the penny rolled fast, and its orbit was wide as it circled around the small hole at the center, but as the penny lost speed, the orbit was drawn tighter and tighter by gravity until the coin disappeared into the hollow. Now imagine a "motorized penny" whose speed you could control. By playing with the velocity, you could keep the penny in a consistent orbit, or you could slow the penny to dive it deep to kiss the chasm. If you chose to accelerate, you could increase the radius of the orbit to bring the coin to the outer limits of the field of play.

This is what motorcycles can do, and it really cannot be experienced in an automobile where negotiating curves is primarily a matter of steering wheel input. But, once a motorcyclist has initiated the turn into a curve, its velocity and lean angle establish an initial *orbit* around the curve. If the curve becomes tighter, backing off the throttle will cause the bike to *fall* tighter into the curve, and the motorcycle turns more sharply. If, on the other hand, the curve becomes less tight (increasing radius), rolling on the throttle increases velocity and will cause the bike to *fall less* into the curve, and with proper throttle modulation, the rider can maintain his relative position on the pavement by forcing the bike away from, or closer to, the inner edge of the curve.

Accelerating at the termination of the curve (where it straightens out) is one of the more thrilling parts of riding a motorcycle, as the bike's lean angle is pressed by centrifugal force back toward the perpendicular so that all is upright again as the motorcycle shoots out of the curve. The wonderful power-to-weight ratio found on larger bikes can make this a very exhilarating experience.

This "altering-your-turn-via-throttle-modulation" is one of three "turning principles" that a rider utilizes in ways unknown to automobile operators. I have spoken elsewhere of the "push-right-to-turn-left" principle of counter-steering so I won't repeat that here, but I will make mention of the third, the "shifting of weight" principle that most of us mastered as children on our first bicycles.

If you've ever ridden a bicycle without hands ("Look, Ma!"), you already know that a two-wheeler can be directionally manipulated and stabilized by adjusting your weight a little this way or that. As you mastered this, you may have even been able to ride no-hands around a corner by shifting just the right amount of weight to one side.

Because of the higher speeds attained on motorcycles, many new riders (or passengers), are reluctant to lean into a curve, not realizing that turning a motorcycle REQUIRES that a certain amount of mass be relocated toward the inside of the curve or corner. The higher the speed coming into the turn, the greater amount of mass that must be transferred, or the curve will simply not be negotiated.

While attending college, I rode a 600cc BMW R60, not a particularly large motorcycle but certainly capable of carrying two people comfortably. My girlfriend and I often enjoyed taking evening rides together, and she was a great passenger, remaining glued to me like a good girlfriend should. Her roommate, having never been on a motor-cycle, pestered me to take her for a ride. Unfortunately, she was a very large gal, profoundly obese, probably pushing 300 pounds. Eventually, my girlfriend insisted that I oblige her friend, and I could no longer avoid it. I twisted the rear coils to their highest preload setting and invited the gal aboard.

We pulled straight ahead from the curb and rode a few blocks with the gal giggling in glee. I signaled for a right turn at an open intersec-tion and began a gentle lean to the right. This startled the gal and she leaned hard to the left out of fear that we were falling. I threw my entire 160 pounds harder to the right, but for every degree of lean angle the Beemer and I were able to achieve, this coed could more than counter in the opposite direction. There was no amount of handlebar manipulation that could force that motorcycle to turn, and so we continued straight ahead as I aborted the attempt. I pulled over and had a chat with my passenger, explaining that unless we intend to circumnavigate the globe in order to return to her dorm, we will have to make some turns, and this would demand that we lean into the curve, or the bike simply will not follow our commands.

I have since made good use of the knowledge that the more mass the rider shifts to the outside of the curve the more the motorcycle itself will have to lean into the curve. Conversely, the more weight the rider shifts to the inside of the curve, the less the motorcycle needs to heel over. I often ride touring motorcycles with limited ground clear-ance for cornering, and I've learned that, by shifting myself to halfway off the saddle toward the inside of the curve (ala a road racer), I can reduce the amount of sparks that fly from parts being ground into the asphalt.

There is really no such thing as "the motorcycling experience." There are simply too many facets to motorcycling for these experi-ences to be described in the singular. But certainly, the *Art of Cornering* ranks among the most mysterious, yet invigorating, aspects of the sport and one that calls out to and continues to challenge even the most seasoned of riders.

My dad and one of his buddies in the early '50s just after a long motorcycle ride that ended up at the airport. Dad is the tall drink of water leaning on the prop of his Aeronca Chief airplane.

Dad flew planes and rode motorcycles well into his retirement years–he even began to fly aerobatic aircraft at age sixty-two.

Dad's aviation background played a key part in adding impact to an observation he once made to me. We had just finished riding along a beautiful stretch of road that tracks the American River in the Sierra Nevada. The road not only snaked left and right in tight S's, but it also rose and fell in concert with the rolling topography. We had pulled over to check our maps and to take a swallow from the canteens when Dad looked back at the road we'd just ran and said, "You know, son. Sometimes riding a motorcycle can be more like flying than flying is like flying."

That statement certainly begged for elaboration, and so I asked him to explain.

He continued, "If you've ever yearned to know what it would feel like to be a bird-swooping up, down, rolling left then right as the wind rushed past your face and body, you can get that sensation better riding roads like this on a motorcycle than you can behind the controls of a typical aircraft."

He went on to explain that most aircraft are enclosed capsules where the sense of speed is diminished the higher you fly. Unless you are engaged in aerobatics or crop-dusting, the dreamed-of sensations of swooping this way and that are not as common for the Cessna pilot as they are for the motorcycle rider.

Dad's observation comes back to me every time I'm riding my bike into a tight, twisty two-laner, particularly when the asphalt's elevation is subject to frequent change. My entire body gets light as I crest a hill, and I can feel my shoulders hunch from increased g-forces as my bike suddenly rises from the bottom of a draw. The curves become less a place I "turn" my bike into and more a place I simply "fall" into as I sway in rhythm with the road. On a motorcycle, I am a falcon tracking the terrain at thirty inches of elevation.

So, with apologies to the few barnstormers and fighter pilots out there, I restate this fact: "Riding a motorcycle is more like flying than flying is like flying."

Trent and I crossed back into New York and made our way to I-90, rolling through Syracuse around sunset. I was surprised by how rural this part of New York was; loaded with dairy farms and agriculture. When you are not from this part of the country, the term "New York" brings to mind only skyscrapers and the Brooklyn Bridge. This ride across this state was a real revelation to me.

We skirted along Lake Erie from Buffalo to the Pennsylvania border. The summer bugs were thick and many of the larger ones were not deflected by the updraft from my windshield, so I had to keep my face shield lowered to keep the critters from peppering me in the face. It called to mind my single-worst experience with getting popped on the head by flying pests at night.

———

One evening while riding through Kansas, I took a bat to the head–not a baseball bat but a bat as in the flying rodent variety. The rear-end of that bat impacted with the forehead of my helmet and rocked my head back so hard I thought I'd have whiplash! As startled as I was by the impact, I can only imagine the surprise that came to the bat as he was cruising along, screaming out into the night, zeroing in on the echoes, and feeling like he was tracking every bug and obstacle in his world. Then WHAP! The poor bat was passed by his own arse! When I got home that night, I wrote a little poem.

Encounter on a Motorcycle

Sonar only warns you of
those things you point it at;
This I realized one dark night
as I rode up the butt of a bat

———

Trent and I stopped for the night at a Pennsylvania town called Northeast. It had been a long day of hard riding and good weather, but the traffic of the greater Boston area and the slow country roads of New Hampshire and Vermont only allowed us to cover a little less than 700 miles. Hopefully, we could open things up as we head across the Rust Belt, the Great Plains, and the wide-open Western states.

CHAPTER 16
DAY NINE

SUNDAY, JUNE 4TH, 2017

Trent and I got another early start, and the traffic was non-existent on the clear Sunday morning as we rode through Erie and into Ohio and through the heart of Cleveland on I-90. Somewhere past Ridgeville, the interstate was under construction. Trent's Buell was on the low side for fuel, but there were no signs warning us that they had placed concrete barriers on both shoulders of the highway that served to block motorists from exiting the interstate for 30 miles. Ten miles into the construction zone, the Buell's low fuel warning light lit up. Ten miles later, with every exit blocked, and within a mile of a state rest area that offered fuel, the Buell ran out of gas. Trent pulled over onto the narrow space between the road edge and the concrete barrier. There was a break in the center barriers near where we had stopped—a place where emergency vehicles could turn around—and these breaks were only spread out every three or four miles. I told Trent to wait in place while I rode ahead to the rest area to buy a gas can so that I could return with fuel.

Fortunately, the rest area sold small gas cans, and I filled it up and strapped it to the Beemer. I then learned that there was no way to access the eastbound lanes without first riding four miles west to the next break in the center barrier. Frustrated by additional delays, I was forced to take this detour. By the time I got to Trent, he had already been interviewed by a state trooper who had just left the scene. We filled the bike and it started up.

I took off with Trent following, but he was riding unusually slow.

He pulled into the rest area a few minutes after I did and reported that the motor had no power, and it seemed to be firing on only one cylinder (it was a two-cylinder engine). I took the bike for a spin, and sure enough, it was only hitting on one lung and could hardly power up to 45 miles per hour.

We pulled off to a side parking lot and unloaded our tools to check for spark, etc. On que, the clouds rolled in, and rain came down on us as we worked on the motor. The plugs both showed good spark, and both cylinders had good compression. I pulled out my phone and surfed the internet for clues as to what was going on. Perhaps the electronic fuel injection needed to be reset since it had run out of gas. I didn't know how to reset this or even if it was possible without proper equipment.

Trent took out his phone and called his brother, Mitch, in Salt Lake City, who also took to his PC in search of answers. Mitch found a 24-hour online motorcycle technician whom he called, and he explained our problem to him. Buells are not a very common motorcycle, and the tech was making some wild guesses, but he gave us a few suggestions. However, nothing he suggested corrected the problem. I had Trent ride the bike for 20 minutes in the large semi-truck parking lot to see if the bike would reset after a couple of miles, but we had no luck.

Trent suggested that we look for a Harley shop, but I reminded him that this was Sunday and that Harley shops are ALWAYS closed on Sundays. He ignored me and did some searching anyway and soon claimed he found a Harley dealer in nearby Sandusky that was open. I told Trent that this must be a typo, but Trent called the number anyway. The phone was answered, and Trent learned that this was Ohio Biker Week and that this was the only Sunday of the year that this dealer was open. He learned that they had techs working that day. I was stunned at the news and couldn't have been happier at being proved wrong.

The shop was 20 miles away, but we reloaded the bikes with our gear and started off. Trouble was, we didn't want to be back on this narrow trough of an interstate with a bike that can't maintain highway speed and at any moment may stop running altogether. I found a narrow opening in the wire fence surrounding the rest area where a pedestrian walkway led to the parking lot for the rest area workers. That parking lot led to the country roads of that area. We squeezed our bikes through the opening in the fence and escaped the interstate.

Trent nursed the Buell down those roads and into Sandusky. When we arrived at the Harley dealership and explained our situation, they immediately put a technician on the case. They pulled the bike into the shop and worked to diagnose the problem. In the meantime, Trent and I noticed that we had arrived during quite the event; the parking lot was filled with tents, featuring parts and accessory vendors and huge "clearance sales" of used motorcycles. There was a radio station broadcasting from the location and food available everywhere. After thirty minutes, the tech reported that there are no error codes reporting and the problem was a mystery to all the techs in the shop, but they were still checking into it. We also learned that the dealership would be closed on Monday (the next day) and will reopen on Tuesday. If they couldn't fix this now, it wouldn't be fixed for at least two more days.

Unfortunately, Trent had to be back to work in Las Vegas on Thursday, and this meant we could not complete the 48 State ride but, rather, we would have to ride directly to Vegas if the repair could not be completed right away.

The techs resumed their investigations while Trent and I discussed the situation. Trent told me to continue the ride without him; that he would fly back to Vegas and then come back for the Buell on a three-day weekend when he had time to ride it back to Nevada. But after all we had been through together, I couldn't bear the thought of finishing the trip without Trent, and I told him that we would find a way.

I then cast my eye on a used Harley Super Glide in the corner of one of the tents. One of the Harley guys who was aware of our entire story helped me work out a deal where they would give me full trade value for the Buell (they were risking that the bike would be easily repaired) AND they would install the windshield and saddlebags from a different used bike onto this Super Glide–all for a very reasonable price difference. It was obvious they were really trying to help us out, and they went above and beyond to get us rolling. By 5:00 p.m., we were again motoring west on the Beemer and the new-to-us Super Glide. We weren't dead yet in our pursuit of the "Stephenson Slam."

We rode past Toledo and into Indiana, skirting the northern border of the state and crossing into Michigan at Sturgis (not the North Dakota Sturgis) to capture Michigan. We dropped back down into Indiana and rode through Gary. We then entered Chicago on the Skyline bridge on a beautiful clear Sunday night, providing a view of the city that was breathtaking. We stopped for the night in the northern suburb of Schaumburg. What a day! 572 miles even with losing half a day of riding time due to a breakdown. We had seen doors open to us with solutions that would not normally have been available to us. It was like a devil was busy trying to thwart our ride, while an angel kept interceding to keep the ride going. Our candle of hope had often been drenched but had never been fully snuffed out.

CHAPTER 17
DAY TEN
MONDAY, JUNE 5TH, 2017

An early start helped Trent and me beat the Chicago area traffic. We headed northwest toward Dubuque, Iowa, but we took a side trip above the Illinois border into Wisconsin at Hazel Green and rode a lovely country road through southwest Wisconsin until we crossed the Mississippi River into Iowa at Dubuque. Trent was on his phone with Mitch quite a bit during gas stops, but that ended when, riding along US 20 in Iowa, I saw Trent's cell phone bounce out of his jacket pocket, rebound off his left saddlebag, and explode into bits and pieces on the asphalt behind his bike. There would be no patching that one back together. I remember thinking as we continued down the highway, *I'll bet I'd just witnessed the disintegration of the largest list of single women's phone numbers in cell phone history*. For the rest of the ride, mine was the only cell phone for reaching the outside world, but we still had our helmet-to-helmet radios for communicating with one another.

We rode through Waterloo and on to Sioux City, crossing the Missouri River into West Sioux City to capture a piece of Nebraska; we then turned around to take I-29 north toward South Dakota. I inadvertently got us heading south on I-29 for a while before Trent realized our mistake, and we spun around to retrace our steps as I muttered disparaging words at myself for wasting precious time on another bone-headed mistake.

We rode north to Sioux Falls, then took a jog to the East on I-90 to capture a piece of Minnesota. This section was under heavy construction, and it took an excruciatingly long amount of time to navigate.

Trent was pushing us hard to make it to Rapid City by day's end. In fact, he was adamant about it.

I still had not taken a turn riding the new Harley. More accurately, Trent had not given me the opportunity. At each gas stop, he continued to decline the offer of my more spacious and luxurious BMW, and I thought, *Boy, that Super Glide must be a sweet ride for him to stick with that all day long.*

Then it dawned on me; for the last few days, even when he was still riding the Buell, Trent had repeatedly declined to switch motorcycles with me. *Was he trying to be nice to the old man by allowing me to remain on the better ride?* I finally asked him to tell me straight up if he was thinking that I needed the softer bike and that I should be given the easier way.

Trent paused before answering, as if he was unsure about how truthful to be. He then replied, "Perhaps that's part of it. You do deserve the cushier ride. But honestly, the main reason is that whoever rides the Beemer has to take lead since the Beemer has the GPS maps and the cruise control to set the pace. And every time you ride on the trailing bike, you tend to call out to me on the radio every little thing that you believe could be a danger that I don't see. 'Watch that guy in the blue truck!' 'Careful not to pass that car until it's really clear!'"

He paused and offered a slight smile to ease the blow, "Dad— you've heard of back seat drivers? Well, you're a back-bike rider! I really do appreciate your concern, but I find it a more pleasant ride to simply follow behind you than to have to hear you in my ear every time I take lead."

We stared at one another for a beat or two as his words sunk in with the weight of the truth. I recalled feeling those same aggravations when I was a sixteen-year-old novice rider on that big ride with my dad and brothers. I resented Dad's frequent advice even though I needed it. But I couldn't recall feeling that way after I became an adult and continued to ride with Dad. I didn't feel that way as an adult because Dad stopped treating me like a novice once I had some real miles behind me. Trent was 32 years old and had ridden around the country just fine by himself for many years now. He didn't need as much as I was dishing out, though that's a hard thing for a caring parent to accept.

I gave a deep sigh, "Tell you what. If I promise to back off on dispensing advice, will you let me have a turn at the Super Glide?" Without a word, Trent walked over to the Beemer and mounted up.

I-90 across North Dakota was surprisingly empty for a summer day when I would have thought there would have been more travelers. This was the wide-open spaces of story and song, and we opened the throttles and flew over the great plains, stopping for gas at a run-down cowboy town that may have been a viable tourist trap twenty years ago. It featured a museum and an old wooden fort, complete with wax Sioux warriors and stuffed bears and buffalo. We only had time to top the tanks and down a cold Dr Pepper, but roadside attractions such as this, barely hanging on in a world of higher-tech entertainment, certainly add color to the journey.

As dusk fell, there were deep shades of crimson and purple in the far western clouds, and the horizon appeared to be further removed than I'd ever seen it. This was truly a land of LOOONG distances, and I thought of how intimidating this vast plain must have looked to those who crossed this on horseback or in wagons.

Our two motorcycle headlights were the sole source of illumination in the moonless night on the unpopulated prairie as the ten o'clock hour rolled around. We seemed to be the only westbound travelers, and the appearance of the occasional semi-truck in the oncoming lanes was getting to be an infrequent occurrence. I was riding the Super Glide when I noticed the headlight modulate in brightness, going from bright to dim and back to bright again. The bike had no voltage gauge, nor did it have an idiot light to indicate the alternator charge, so I had little clue what was going on with the electrical system. I radioed to Trent, asking him to pull in behind me and tell me if the taillight was also modulating in brightness. He confirmed that it was fluctuating between bright and dim, and I deduced that I had either a bad alternator or a bad battery. I recalled that the Harley dealer had to jump start the bike when we purchased it the previous day, but we all assumed that this was because the bike had sat idle for some time. I now figured that the bike was running solely on whatever juice was remaining in the weak battery, and any remaining power could run out at any time. We were in the middle of nowhere with no city lights on any horizon. Modern bikes do not give you the option of turning off the running lights to conserve power, so we just had to ride on and hope for the best.

When we finally arrived at the next exit, it was for the town of

Kadoka, and we reached it about fifteen minutes after discovering our problem. There was a gas station/convenience store just off the exit and we pulled in. We left the motor on and checked all the wiring connections before shutting it down. I noticed that when I idled the motor I had full lights, but when I revved the engine, the lights faded, *weird*.

I turned the bike off then attempted a restart, and sure enough, it wouldn't fire. It was 11:00, and we were stuck for at least the night in what seemed to me to be a *nothing town* in the middle of the prairie. I asked the station attendant if there was a parts store in Kadoka, and he replied that there was only a tractor shop.

It once again appeared that our 48-state odyssey was doomed. Even with another half-day delay, we could not complete the circuit within ten days of riding, and we would probably have to abandon the capturing of Idaho, Washington, and Oregon in favor of taking a direct route home so that Trent could return to work on time.

While I had an awareness that this setback was likely the final nail in the coffin, I was still desperately searching my mind for options and solutions. We had found miracles at many junctures on this journey, but it appeared that our Cinderella ride was nearing midnight and that the magic would die with the Super Glide's battery in Kadoka, South Dakota.

While I was grilling the station attendant for information that might, somehow lead to some resolution, or at least, some *hope* for an answer, Trent had taken my phone and called his brother, Mitch, who lives over 500 miles away from our location. Mitch had been helpful over the phone the previous day as we tried to diagnose the problem on the Buell. Trent was explaining our troubles to Mitch, but I ignored their conversation, failing to see how Mitch could assist us this time around. I overheard Trent ask Mitch if there was a parts store open at this time of night in Rapid City (still 110 miles away) as I went back into the service station to borrow some needed tools.

When I got back outside, Trent handed me the phone and said, "Dad, you need to talk to Mitch." Still preoccupied with thinking of a solution, I annoyingly grabbed the phone and uttered a curt, "Hey, Mitch. What's up?"

Mitch reported that he had found a battery at a 24-hour Walmart in Rapid City. My mind immediately calculated how long it would take me to ride the Beemer to Rapid City and back. I figured that this would likely be a 4-hour round-trip if I could stay awake that long. Mitch then said "Dad, I'll have the battery to you in an hour and a half."

My mind spun–this made no sense. "Dad," Mitch continued, "I'm in Rapid City."

I could not process this... "What? You're in Rapid City? How can that be?"

Mitch then revealed that he, Trent, and Mom had plotted to have him surprise me by riding his Suzuki Intruder to rendezvous with us in Rapid City to join us for the final two days.

I was gobsmacked. Just when the wonders and marvels of this odyssey had appeared fully exhausted, it was "Mitchie to the rescue!"

I sent him the details for the needed part. He told me he only had 20% remaining on his phone battery, and his motorcycle's fuel tank only had a range of 90 miles. I told him to refuel midway, at around the 50- or 60-mile mark because there was not much out this way and that he should conserve his phone battery by turning it off as he rode so that he could power it back up in case of problems.

We hung up, and I thought about finding us a place to stay for the night. It was 11:30 when I left Trent at the station to watch over the Harley while I rode the Beemer into the town. As I rode, I noticed lightning flashing to the west where Mitch would be coming from, and I shook my head and offered a silent prayer, *oh, please don't send Mitch a rainstorm!*

I was the sole motorist on the main street of Kadoka, and all the businesses were dark. I tried the first mom-and-pop motel I came to, but the office was locked, and no one responded to repeated attempts on the doorbell. I saw another old motel that had four rusted hulks of cars sitting in the gravel parking lot, and the motel appeared to be open. I entered the front door, but no one could be found. I called out and even walked the halls, unsure if this dilapidated motel was even in operation, but I couldn't find a soul. It was like the rapture had occurred, and I was the only living mortal around.

I rode further into town, and by now, the lightning was very intense to the west and the wind had picked up considerably. I was getting very concerned about Mitch riding through it. I found another 1950s style motel and rang the bell until a woman appeared. I was able to secure a room. I rode the Beemer to the front door of the room and unloaded the gear from the bike. Only one other vehicle sat in the parking lot, an old Chevy with Kansas plates.

By the time I got back to Trent, the weather was pretty bad with sheets of rain and gusting winds. Most concerning for me were the constant flashes of lightning to the west, knowing that motorcycles do not enjoy the same *immunity* from fatal lightning strikes that automobiles do, and that my six-foot-four youngest son was a relatively tall target riding along that empty freeway on a desolate plain. I sent Mitch a text instructing him to please remain in place wherever he stops for gas and to NOT proceed in the storm. I knew that he was unlikely to read the text since he had powered down his phone, and even if it was turned on, it would likely be buried in the pocket of his hefty leathers and the message would go unnoticed. Besides, as Trent pointed out, Mitch relishes the opportunity to help others and would be prone to disregard his own welfare for the sake of someone who he felt was counting on him. Trent and I went to the side of the station and offered a prayer that Mitch would be safe.

When we returned to the front of the station, we huddled under the protection of an awning over a picnic table to wait for Mitch's arrival. Trent told me that, while I was gone, a man, apparently a local, had pulled up to the gas pumps in an old truck, stepped out mumbling incoherently, and, spotting Trent sitting next to his Harley, staggered toward Trent, who immediately realized the guy was sauced. The man looked down at Trent and said he was going to give him a whoopin'. Trent is a tad over six-foot tall himself and owns a gold medal in boxing from the Utah Summer Games. Trent stood up, looked the man in the eye, and simply replied "Really?" The man thought better of it, spun on his heels, and left. Again, I was taken aback by the Twilight Zone kind of stuff going on in this town.

We continued working on the bikes to keep our minds occupied because we, or more accurately I, had a terrible feeling about Mitch riding out this storm. Trent stated confidently that he was sure that Mitch would be okay, but despite the many miracles we'd seen up to this point, my irrepressible cynicism responded, "He'll be okay, only if our luck changes."

A little after 1:00 in the morning, I heard the sweetest exhaust note that has ever greeted this father's ear. I jumped to my feet and ran into the parking lot as Mitch, fully decked out in rain gear and drenched to the bone, came riding up with a huge grin on his face. I couldn't control my emotions as raindrops blended with tears, and both Trent and I bear-hugged the boy like he had just liberated Paris.

We installed the battery and the bike fired right up with no signs of faltering in the lights. I still didn't have the meter to test the charging system, and I knew we couldn't leave Kadoka until we were certain this was resolved. There were still a lot of empty prairies to cover, and we needed to know that the Super Glide would keep its charge across those vast distances. But, for now, we had new life again. We re-packed the bikes and rode to the hotel where we collapsed at 2:00 am.

I later learned that Mitch had ridden 700 miles that day, riding from Salt Lake City, through the Wyoming backroads past Devil's Gate and Independence Rock to arrive at Rapid City. Trent and Mitch's plan had been to have Mitch positioned on an overpass, and when he saw us riding through, Mitch would take the onramp to ride up beside us and then see how long it took for me to realize that it was my own baby boy riding alongside. For them, this was the most eagerly anticipated point of the trip. While things didn't go down as they had planned, it seemed that Heaven writes better scripts than do mortals and, in retrospect, we wouldn't have changed a thing. It was "The Perfect Rendezvous."

CHAPTER 18
DAY ELEVEN

TUESDAY, JUNE 6TH, 2017

I had set my alarm for 6:00, figuring I'd let the boys sleep while I went to that tractor repair shop the station attendant mentioned, hoping they would have the meter I needed to test the Harley's charging system. In the motel parking lot, I spotted the only other guest of the motel, an older gentleman smoking a cigarette while leaning on that Chevy from Kansas. He saw me and shuffled over to talk about the motorcycles. As I loaded an item or two into the saddlebags, he told me that he used to ride a Triumph Tiger "back in the day," and I shook my head in partially-sincere appreciation as he told me a story or two. As I donned my jacket and swung my leg over the Harley, he asked where I was heading so early in the morning. I told him that I was going to the tractor shop to see if they had the meter that I needed to test my charging system. He took another drag on his cigarette, blew out a stream of smoke and replied, "Oh, I carry one of those with me when I travel–you know; just in case."

My gloved hand froze just as I was about to insert the key into the ignition. I turned my helmeted head to the old man. "Are you kidding me?" I asked incredulously.

I just had to chuckle with a mixture of amazement and gratitude when the old boy pulled out of his trunk the very tool I needed. We tested the system, and it was charging properly. It had only been a battery problem, and we had now corrected that.

Rather than go back to bed to catch a few more minutes of rest, I spent some time sending a report to our Facebook followers, telling them of our wild previous day and of our "unexpected angel" in the form of our rain-soaked Mitch. All through this journey it had been "challenge, followed by amazing miracles, followed by another challenge, and another open door." Somehow, we kept stumbling forward with renewed hope that we would be able to complete the ride. We packed and made ready to ride into the rain (of course).

There was something so "exactly right" about riding in formation with both of my two sons. The team was so much more complete. The Suzuki Intruder that Mitch rode had a smaller fuel tank, and we had to stop for fuel more frequently. We all rotated between the three bikes at each gas stop, and I turned the navigation planning over to the boys for the rest of the trip. The two seem to relish contending with their sibling over which would be the best plan. Amazingly, they always ended up concurring no matter who originated the eventual solution.

The rain was light and didn't last long. The ride into Rapid City was beautiful as the shadows of the dispersing clouds cast their enchantment onto the topography in Badlands territory. We continued on I-90 through Sturgis (the "real" one) and Spearfish and then turned around one exit after crossing the Wyoming border ("tag you're it"). We retraced our steps to Spearfish then headed north on US 85 to ride through Belle Fourche, Redig, and Buffalo before crossing the border into North Dakota to catch US 12 West. We entered Montana just 12 miles east of Baker.

Perhaps because we had so recently crossed so many of the smaller eastern states in a very short amount of time, I found myself surprised by how long it took to traverse the state of Montana, even at elevated highway speeds. Every time we'd stop for gas, and we'd pull out the map to check our progress, our relative advancement on the page was minuscule. None of us had any complaints about the scenery; it's a gorgeous state. But when your focused eye is cast on the far border, Montana seemed to be the most time-consuming state of our entire journey. I eased the monotony by thinking back on the last time I had ridden across the Big Sky Country.

———

It was on the "graduation trip" that Mitch and I took at the end of his senior year. We were on the return leg of a 4,000-mile ride and were heading west through Montana on US 2 just a little south of the Canadian border. This was primarily a two-lane highway that connected one farm town to another, and in between settlements, we kept our speeds up around 80 mph if we felt we could get away with it. Since I was the one who planned the routes, it was not unusual for me to take lead, though Mitch remained close in my rearview mirrors.

On one particular stretch of highway, we were rolling along at a good rate when I noticed Mitch fading back farther and farther until I couldn't see him any longer in my mirrors. I pulled over and paused, then turned my bike around to see what had delayed him.

I found him stopped on the side of the highway with his helmet off. I came to a stop on the shoulder on the opposite side of the road and noticed he was working on his bandanna.

He called out to me, "My bandanna kept sliding down over my eyes until I couldn't see. I got tired of trying to poke it back in place under my helmet."

Mitch and I both had the same practice of wearing a bandanna as a "doo-rag," covering our heads under our helmets. At each gas stop we would wet these down and they then served as "evaporative coolers" on our heads as we rode (it also greatly reduces helmet-itch). I thought it strange that Mitch's bandanna could slide forward to cover his eyes when it is strapped securely into place between his skull and the helmet. Besides, we had ridden over 3000 miles so far without this problem, so I didn't understand why the issue would now arise.

I wheeled my Hog behind the Sportster, and his rear tire caught my eye. I wondered, *was his bike settled deep into the dirt or was his tire going flat?* I dismounted to investigate, and with both motorcycles now shut down, I could clearly hear the hissing as air escaped the rear tire.

Side note: In 1975, when I was 17 years old, my dad and I rode a Honda 750 from Kansas City, Missouri, to Cape Canaveral, Florida. Dad did most of the riding while I sat perched behind him on the rear seat. A little south of Memphis, passing a semi-truck on a downhill at high speed, the rear tire on our motorcycle blew out. Suddenly, at better than 75 miles an hour, the rear of the Honda walked its way to the right. Dad kept the front wheel pointed straight ahead and rode it like a dirt-tracker in a power-slide until the bike was somewhat sideways to our direction of travel. Just as the forks were about to lock, the flat tire flapping around on the rim walked the bike around to the left and Dad again kept the motorcycle straight despite what the rear-end of the bike had in mind. All the while, I was flagging to the semi-truck driver bearing down on us from behind to slow down because we were in serious trouble. I could hear the truck's applied air brakes as the driver downshifted. Dad managed to get the motorcycle to a stop on the right shoulder. It was a harrowing experience, and I was glad my dad was at the controls when it happened. Even as a cocky teenager, I could sense that there is no substitute for experience in situations like that, and a younger rider like me might not have saved the day. This was the only time, in all my years of riding, that I have experienced a tire blowout at full speed.

Mitch and I crouched down behind the Sportster and found the nail hole in the center of the tread. Among the tools I carry with me on long rides is a tire plug kit and a can of Fix-A-Flat. Within fifteen minutes, we were again on the road, with me riding the Sportster in case the repairs didn't take.

Later that night, Mitch and I spoke about how incredible a "coincidence" it was that we stopped when we did. We recounted:

- I've ridden all my life using the "wet bandanna under the helmet trick" and I've never had one come loose to impede my vision. Neither had Mitch, including in the ten days we'd been riding on this trip.
- We had ridden 3000 miles up to that point, and at the very mile that the tire received the injury that could have put

Mitch down at high speed, his bandanna came loose and demanded he pull over to fix it.

We decided that, though we don't know the top speed at which an angel can fly, on that day, in northern Montana, we clocked one doing 80 miles an hour as he unloosed Mitch's do-rag and pulled it down over his eyes.

———

My reminiscing over past rides ceased as Trent signaled he needed gas. We stopped for lunch in a typical cow town and pulled into the gravel parking lot of the local ma-and-pop burger joint. There was a walk-up window and an awning that covered the outdoor dining area, consisting of six picnic tables and a couple of oil drums-turned-into-garbage cans. The staff was composed of three females: one of them in her teens, one in her twenties, and one who appeared in her mid thirties. As he always does, Trent went out of his way to obtain their names and he used the names as he placed his order and asked about their day. This flirtation was very well received by this trio, and they returned to the order window repeatedly to further the conversation. They seemed keenly interested in our trip, but it was all too apparent that they were really enamored by Trent. Their skillful interrogation revealed Trent's age and that he was single. They would then retreat for a bit, we'd hear giggles, and they would then return with more questions. They asked if they could subscribe to our Facebook page, and Trent gave them the site name. I asked Trent if it seemed unusual to be treated like a rock star with groupies and he shrugged, replying in his slightly annoying, cock-sure Trent-way: "Nah; not that unusual."

Trent and Mitch pored over the maps, and I took a photo that I really love that shows the two making their plans like they have so often done throughout their lives.

Though I was certain we'd be able to overnight in Butte or even stretch the night to reach Missoula, we found ourselves calling it a night 45 miles west of Billings at Columbus. We found a comfortable old motel where they had a *suite* of sorts with three beds. There was a convenience store attached that was about to close, and we refilled our saddlebag supplies, knowing that the next day would have to be the longest ride of the entire trip, 1100 miles, if we were to complete the ride within ten days of actual riding (we'd lost two days due to mechanical issues). Trent had called into work and bought a couple of days of latitude, so at least he was not going to get fired for our tardy arrival. Our new completion deadline was 7:31 a.m. on Thursday morning. If we could do that, Trent and I would complete the 48 State circuit in ten days of riding.

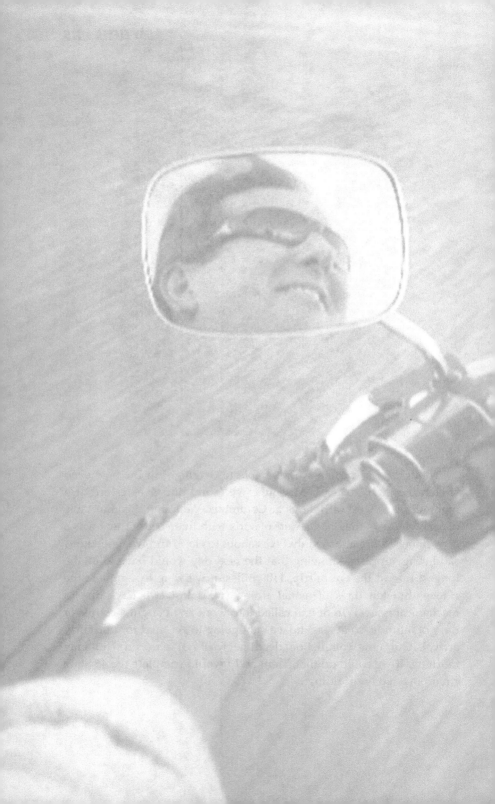

CHAPTER 19

DAY TWELVE
WEDNESDAY, JUNE 7TH, 2017

We had two route choices for the final day. We could continue on I-90 northwest to cross the Idaho panhandle and into Spokane, WA, then turn south to pick up a piece of eastern Oregon before slicing southeast across Idaho and into Utah. This is the longer route but enjoys better highways with faster speeds. Or we could venture across Idaho on winding two-lane state roads that offer a more direct attack but are likely much slower for travel. We debated for a bit, and the boys chose the two-laners.

We left Columbus at the crack of dawn, traveling on I-90 to Missoula where we caught highway 12 southwest, crossing the continental divide as we entered Idaho. The road followed the Lochsa River from the Bitterroot National Forest into the Nez Percé National Forest. The torrid river remained just to the left of the road as both the water and the pavement snaked its way through the hills. Traffic was light, and we were able to maintain a fairly brisk pace.

At one point, there was a broad pull-out and parking lot adjacent to the river. There were bathrooms and a series of ramps designed for sliding large river rafts from the parking lot to the riverbank. Mitch thought it would be fun to slide himself down these ramps, and he did, challenging me to do the same. It looked fun, so I followed suit.

This was a big mistake! I landed hard on my tailbone at the first *landing*, and this bothered me considerably for the rest of the ride and for a month thereafter. Of course, I tried to talk Trent into taking the slide, but he was too wise for that.

We turned northwest at Kooskia and rode through Orofino and Lenore, crossing the Snake River into Washington state at Clarkston. We once again retraced our steps to the east to hit US 95 south through Craigmont and Grangeville. This was beautiful country with grand rolling foothills carpeted in the ordered rows of agriculture. The road descended to run beside the Little Salmon River by White Bird, and we continued clear through to Weiser where we again crossed the Snake River, this time to enter Oregon. We caught I-84 which would be our final highway to take us back across Idaho and south into Utah.

The sun was setting as we entered Idaho. We had promised my niece, Marisa, and her family that we would stop by to see them when we came through Boise, and we were anxious to see the kids again–a really great family. I called ahead and arranged to meet them at a McDonalds just off one of the exits in Boise. We had a nice rest, told them all about our adventures, took a bunch of photos, and then headed back out on the highway.

The night was clear but very dark. There was no moon in the early evening and few towns or cities to add any degree of illumination. An enormous detour near Twin Falls had us heading north for twenty miles, then east on Hwy 24 for 50 miles before rejoining the interstate near Rupert. This was a painfully slow and congested detour, and we didn't get back to the main road until well after midnight.

Once we were back on the interstate, we opened things up. For the most part, it was just three motorcycles, an empty highway, and an enormous black sky. We were on the northeast rim of the Great Basin, and I couldn't help recalling a similar night, decades before, when I crossed the Great Basin from the west.

———

In the summer following my freshman year in college, I decided to take a solo ride on my BMW from my parent's home in Las Vegas to see a gal I'd dated at school. After a three-day visit with my lady-friend, I headed back out for the return trip, planning to make camp for the night at Mono Lake. I arrived at the lake at around 10:00 that evening, but I was not feeling sleepy so I pushed on, (my 19-year-old body could do things I can no longer imagine standing up to). I hit Big Pine at 11:30 and topped my tank for the long ride across the desolate Lida Road, a western entrance to the vast and foreboding Great Basin. Next gas was 134 miles away in Beatty, Nevada.

The Lida Road is an empty stretch of asphalt on its busiest day, and on this moonless night, I never saw another vehicle for two hours. Once I was 30 minutes out of Big Pine, I never even saw the glimmer of a single lightbulb glowing anywhere in the distance. The desert held nothing more than scrub brush, scattered boulders, and abandoned ghost towns.

At one point, the road snakes through a shallow canyon with its rim only twenty feet above the road on either side. Rounding a curve, I spotted a large coyote on the road ahead of me, and he scurried into the brush before I arrived at the point where he left the road. Alone in the dark, my teenage mind questioned whether that was actually a coyote. Could it have been a wolf? If it was a wolf, don't they travel in packs? I imagined a dozen lobos running just above me on the rim of this shallow canyon where the tight switchbacks kept me from exiting second gear to put some distance between me and the (hopefully) imagined wolfpack tracking me from above. When the road straightened, I eagerly reached for higher gears and felt that thrill that comes from escaping danger, a thrill just as real even if the threat was only imagined. At 2:00 a.m., I rolled into Beatty and was pleased to find an all-night gas station in this humble little town. I was also pleased to still feel no fatigue or sleepiness.

Rolling south on US 95 in the wee hours of the morning, I was once again the only vehicle on the highway. No moon, no towns, no lights in any direction except for the limited tunnel of a yellow beam projecting forward from my meager six-volt headlamp.

This is when I experience what cannot be matched in the confines of a car. With no roof above me and with no clouds in the sky, the Milky Way had never revealed itself in greater majesty. I was in my own personal planetarium, and it stretched from horizon to horizon in perfect clarity. As I rocked back my helmet to drink in the sight, two shooting stars simultaneously flared brilliantly in parallel paths, looking like the bright sparks from a welder's striker as he lights his torch. I drew in a quick breath and quickly thought of a wish I could make. And then another flash streaked across the sky, followed almost immediately by yet another.

Each year in August, The Perseid Meteor Shower comes to the northern hemisphere. Though my rendezvous with this astronomical wonder was unplanned, the shower became a firework show staged exclusively for me. The science almanacs report that, at its climax, the Perseid meteors flare the sky at a rate of around one per minute. What I experienced on that desert highway on that early morning was at least twice that. I made so many wishes on falling stars that I'm sure the angels lost count. It was the most amazing celestial display I could ever hope to witness.

Photo taken on Lida Road ten or more years after my solo ride across this stretch. My dad and my friend Scott Doney joined me for a ride to Yosemite.

————

Trent, Mitch, and I made a turn southward at the split from I-86 and we were then on our final leg. There were virtually no other motorists on the highway at the late hour of 2:00 a.m. Trent and I kept checking over the radios to see if the other guy was still alert and still feeling good. We did the same through hand signals to Mitch. We all had to stay sharp. I had had a chilling experience with what can happen when cobwebs sink in and a motorcycle leaves the highway.

————

Of all my motorcycle-related stories, there is one I am most hesitant to share with others. It is intensely personal and of a nature that it may be best reserved for my most trusted of friends, and so I have debated including it in this narrative of my motorcycle journeys. Of all I have witnessed in this life, what I am about to relate is one of those experiences where the reader really needs to have been there on-site when this occurred to fully appreciate it. I will retell the chain of events as I experienced them, knowing that the skeptic may scoff but that the perceptive will understand.

On the ides of March 1991, my mother, Billye, and my father, "Big Jim," arose early and had breakfast together in their Las Vegas home before Dad headed out for a morning meeting. Just an hour or two later, Dad returned to the house to find my mother slumped motionless on the living room couch, the morning paper still resting on her lap. At age 55, Mom had suffered a massive heart attack, and despite Dad's desperate efforts, he couldn't bring her back to us.

On that morning, Dad's foundations seemed to crumble as this former tower of strength revealed just how much our mother had been his bedrock. He wept, he embraced us in his arms in a manner unfamiliar to us, or at least, to our family customs. He spoke tenderly and frequently of his love, not only for Mom, but for each of us. He seemed lost and unsure—he could barely function in daily activities; he didn't sleep, and he hardly ate. We waited for our powerful patriarch to rise again, to lead us through our grief, but even after the funeral, there was little sign of the confident and unflappable man we had known.

As a God-fearing Christian, Dad didn't doubt that Heaven was in charge and that Mom was in a better place, but he still felt an ache for an assurance that Mom was okay. He yearned for a chance to say a proper goodbye. He had heard stories of people who, after losing a loved one, were blessed with a dream or vision wherein the departed visited them as an opportunity was afforded for a final exchange of sentiments. He spoke repeatedly of his desire for this, and he even prayed that God would grant him such an experience. He and I discussed his wish, and he acknowledged that we could never develop the true faith that we were put on this earth to gain if God were to grant a peek beyond the veil to every mourner who had been left behind in mortality. Still, he wanted just one more exchange between he and his treasured Billye.

A few weeks after the funeral, my riding buddy, Scott Doney, and I were discussing our concerns about Dad's emotional state, which by this time, was even affecting his physical condition. We felt that Dad needed to get away from the house where reminders of Mom lurked around every corner. We felt that what Dad really needed was to get away for a motorcycle ride, something that had always soothed his soul. We asked him to join us on a ride to Tombstone, Arizona, and he accepted.

Wanting to get an early start, Scott and I arrived at Dad's house at 5:30 on the morning of the ride, Scott riding his blue BMW R75 and me riding my red Harley Electra Glide. Dad was already up and in his garage, loading his Electra Glide, which was also red and a match to my bike. When asked how he'd slept, his only answer was a dismissive "Well, you know."

We rolled south out of Vegas on U.S. 95 to Laughlin, where we caught a bite of breakfast. Crossing the Colorado River, we followed the eastern shore through Havasu, Parker, and Quartzsite before turning east on I-10. At an afternoon gas stop somewhere in the valley separating the Harquahala Mountains from the Gila Bend range, we paused to quench our thirsts.

It was late Spring, but the desert was not cutting us a break, and we peeled off our outer layer of leathers and watered down our bandannas to help cool our necks. As Dad and I found shade on the porch of an outbuilding, Scott took a snapshot of father and son with our matching motorcycles—a photo that very nearly captured my father's final hour.

We continued east to Phoenix where I-10 turns south toward Tucson, and by 3:00 in the afternoon, we had passed Casa Grande. I was riding lead when I heard Dad's Big Red roll up from behind. Pulling along flank, he shouted, "I'm sleepy! Let's pull over!" I motioned for him to take lead, and I settled in behind.

The next exit was for the town of Eloy, and Dad's turn signals told us this was his rest stop. He leaned his Harley into the gentle curve of the exit as I trailed him by thirty yards, while Scott followed a hundred yards behind me. I saw Dad's helmet turn to the left and I assumed he was looking beyond the upcoming overpass, searching for the best gas station to take a break. I could see that the curve of the offramp became significantly sharper to the right just in front of Dad, and when his helmet did not return to center, I knew that a drowsiness had set in–he was foggy-headed and rolling fast toward trouble.

I shouted, "DAD! WATCH OUT!" It was a useless scream against the howl of the wind and roar of the engines. Dad's tires hit the narrow ribbon of gravel skirting the asphalt and Dad's helmet snapped back around as he was jolted awake. He dove his right shoulder deep into the curve and tried to get the Hog to follow. A spray of pea gravel shot upward, but the bike couldn't hold the curve against the loose footing as man and machine, at over fifty miles an hour, descended into the shallow depression of desert that spread between the offramp and the freeway.

As I cut hard into the curve on my own motorcycle, I watched to my left as my father fought the 750-lb machine that bucked and twisted below him like a Brahman bull. All at once, the front forks jerked violently to the left and Big Jim and Big Red disappeared into a great ball of dust, rocks, and flying bits of mesquite. Within this compact dust devil, I saw the machine roll over Dad at least once.

I locked my brakes and slid my Harley to a stop on the asphalt perpendicular to the roiling cloud of dirt. Not bothering to lower my kickstand, I dropped my bike to the ground and ran toward the scene. As the dust settled, I found Dad lying on his back, his eyes open, fixed, and full of dirt. I checked for breath and pulse but found nothing. Scott arrived soon after, and we administered CPR as we screamed at Dad to breathe.

While trying to resuscitate him, I couldn't help but think of my five brothers and our baby sister. How could I tell them, weeks after losing our mother, that we had just lost Dad?

Other motorists stopped and came to assist. We continued our efforts until someone shouted that they saw Dad blink, then close his eyes. We ceased our efforts and could see his chest rise and fall ever so slightly. He then coughed once or twice. His eyes remained closed, but his lips worked in an effort to speak. As his breath got stronger his mumbles evolved to distinct words, and his head shook left then right as if signaling he was unhappy with what we were doing. Scott and I leaned in closer to hear what he wanted.

"Billye!" he mouthed with desperation in his voice, "Where are you going! Come back! Don't leave me here! Wait, wait for me–don't go!"

Scott and I shot each other a glance. I leaned closer, "Dad, is Mom here?"

His eyes remained closed as he continued to call her name and to plead with her not to leave him behind. Then, as if he left another world to return to ours, his eyes fluttered open, and he ceased calling for Mom. He moaned about his injuries, calling out different body parts that were in pain.

Paramedics soon arrived and assessed his condition. They called for a helicopter, and within what seemed like only minutes, a Flight-for-Life chopper landed on the asphalt next to my Harley. It was then that I noticed that a kind stranger had righted my Harley and placed it on its kickstand.

Despite what you see in the movies, they don't allow family members to accompany injured loved ones on the helicopters. They simply told me which hospital Dad would be taken to, and then they flew away, leaving Scott and I to deal with the broken Harley and to make our own way to the hospital in Phoenix.

After a tow truck hauled away Dad's motorcycle and the State Trooper finished questioning us, Scott and I had a moment to ourselves.

"Did you see what I saw?" Scott asked.

I nodded, "She came for him, didn't she?"

"Sure looked like it," Scott responded.

Again, I nodded, "Well, we're not ready to give him up yet."

We started our motorcycles and headed back north toward Phoenix and the hospital. Once at the medical center, we found that Dad was still being attended to and assessed. They knew he had broken several ribs, that he had a severe concussion, and they were not yet certain about the internal injuries. He was sedated, and they did not want to bring him back to consciousness until the following day.

Scott and I checked into a nearby motel, and I called my siblings to inform them of the accident. My brother, Monte, booked a flight to join us early in the morning. Before going to bed, Scott and I again rehearsed the whole episode and reached a few conclusions:

First, we shouldn't have pressed Dad to ride so far when he'd been sleeping so poorly the past few weeks, though neither of us imagined that Big Jim could ever fall asleep in the saddle.

Second, Scott and I had both always believed that there was a very thin veil between this world and the next, but that day, we had witnessed someone teeter between both spheres. In one moment, Dad spoke to those on one side, and in the next, he became aware of his temporal state and returned his focus to us. We were anxious to hear of this experience from Dad's own lips.

The next morning, we picked up my brother at the airport and rode to the hospital. Dad was kept sedated throughout the morning, and the doctors told us he was badly battered but would survive to endure a lengthy recovery period.

When Dad awakened, his grogginess wore off quickly, and we were able to talk about the accident. He remembered signaling to take the exit, and he remembered the few seconds of riding rodeo on his steel stallion, but he recalled nothing else until he awoke in the hospital. We asked him about those moments as he lay in the dirt next to his bike, and he only shook his head. We told him of having to perform CPR and of the words he mumbled as he came back to us. Dad sat up a bit in his bed and anxiously leaned forward asking us to repeat every detail. His eyes filled with a mixture of hope and dismay as we told him again what we witnessed. We could see him trying to force himself to remember those moments, to recall seeing my mom there with him, to know that she was close by and waiting for him. He asked us once more to repeat every word of what he'd said and what we'd seen.

Though frustrated that he could not recall the experience, he took great solace in our words, which in the end, simply declared *our* witness of *his* witness of the reality of life after death and of the continued association with our loved ones. God seemed to have found a way to provide Dad with the answer to his prayer for a sign that all was well with his dear Billye while still requiring Dad to accept this on faith.

Big Red suffered no damage to frame nor engine, but virtually every other part was bent, crushed, or shattered. A few months later, the bike was put back into like-new condition. On the other hand, Dad took a bit longer, but he eventually healed, both body and soul, and returned to ride Big Red for another dozen years before Alzheimer's took that joy away from him. Dad has since passed on to experience that grand reunion once again. A reunion that he once briefly glimpsed as he lay heart-broken and body-broken in the desert sand near Eloy, Arizona.

————

Having seen what those *cobwebs* can do, even to the most experienced of riders when drowsiness overwhelms the will to press on, I signaled to Trent, just as I promised I would, and then followed him off the freeway at Exit 283, Juniper Road. The wind sprints that Trent did with me got my blood to flowing and the cool Gatorade worked to refresh my wits. But Trent still didn't push me. That was also part of our pact. Even being this close, less than a dozen miles between us and the border, between us and achieving our goal, Trent and I were willing to stop right here rather than risk the unthinkable.

The hypnosis induced during the past hours by the monotony and consistency of this straight strip of freeway, illuminated before us for only fifty yards at a time, was finally fading as my *second wind* gained strength. We still waited another ten minutes after I felt ready to ride, until I was sure, and Trent and Mitch were sure, that the spell had been broken.

"Alright–I'm good now," I told the boys. "Let's ride. Next stop, Snowville."

It was 3:00 a.m. Trent and I kept a conversation going as Trent wanted to keep me alert. I didn't think I really needed it anymore, but I appreciated it, nonetheless.

The road was absolutely empty under a rising June moon when me and the boys lined our bikes up three abreast on the two southbound lanes, wanting to cross the Utah border–our finish line–together.

Me and my boys. Me and my wingmen. Trent, whose ever-calm demeanor and self-assured confidence had kept us steadily marching toward our goal. Mitch, whose eagerness to be a part of all this had brought him to just the right place at just the right time to do what he so loves to do: to be of service, to be of use, to be the answer to someone else's dilemma. As the three of us rode past the Utah welcome sign, we blew our horns and shouted our fool heads off! I could easily imagine any nearby coyotes raising their heads in bewilderment as we passed by.

We had completed the 48 State circuit in less than twelve actual days and in less than ten riding days. Perhaps not good enough for the Iron Butt Association, but certainly satisfying to us. As Rocky Balboa might say "Ain't gonna be no rematch!" We'd proven all we needed to prove.

There were no motels available at Snowville, so we rode another few miles until we found a ranch road exit where we pulled the bikes into a cow pasture and spread a tarp between motorcycles as a makeshift tent. Such shelters had become almost a tradition with the Stephenson family.

| *Dad and Clamett's camp in Mexico in 1953.*

Dad and I pull a tarp between Harleys in 1988.

Me and the boys and our camp at the conclusion of our 48-
state odyssey

In the morning, we broke camp, and each of us got onto our own
bikes. We rode together until we were nearly to Salt Lake City where
Mitch and I peeled off to I-80 while Trent continued south for Las

Vegas. Mitch and I then separated at Bangerter Highway, he rode west to Tooele, and I went to report in at a branch office my company kept in Salt Lake City.

I let out a long sigh as Mitch peeled off. This grand adventure had concluded. And already I wondered what would come next. What would be our next motorcycle adventure?

CHAPTER 20
A TRIBUTE

I started this book with the story of my feeble and fading father giving me the gift of a motorcycle. Through the subsequent chapters, I've tried to share what a gift that has been throughout my life. Though there are still more roads to ride and additional memories to make in the years to come, I want to close this account with a tribute to my dad, a tribute that you may now be better equipped to understand.

Dad passed away in that convalescence center where we had taken that final photograph, the two of us leaning against that big silver Harley. He was surrounded by family who spent the final hours whispering to Dad their words of gratitude for all he had done for them and for all that he had left them with.

Though Dad died in Cedar City, Utah, his funeral was held in Las Vegas, Nevada, where he had spent the final thirty years of his life, where he had built a successful business, and where most of his children, grandchildren, and great-grandchildren still resided. For my brothers, sisters, and our friends, it just wouldn't do for Dad to take that three-hour hearse ride unaccompanied, so we arranged for a motorcycle escort, composed of family and friends, to lead his hearse on the journey.

Eight riders on six motorcycles comprised Dad's procession, including three of his sons, one daughter, one son-in-law, two of his friends, and his wife, Laura. Dad had been a private pilot and a vice president of a major international airline, and so we wore matching

vintage TWA shirts reading "Wing Man" to remind ourselves that this
ride was the least we could do for him, who had always *had our six*.

I rode out front on Big Red, Dad's final motorcycle, with Dad's
widow, Laura, (my saintly and adventuresome stepmother), occu-
pying the saddle behind me just as she had with Dad in the final
decade and a half of his life. With blue skies above and dry pavement
beneath, it was a perfect final ride.

The funeral was held a day or two later. The chapel was packed as
his amazing life was eulogized with tributes coming in from captains
of major industries and from simple riding buddies from as far away
as Australia. Dad was a Bronze Star recipient for action he saw in the
Pacific during WWII, and it was a moving moment when Laura was
presented with the tightly folded flag from his casket, accompanied
with words of appreciation from a grateful nation.

The mortuary gave us permission to pull Big Red up to the burial
site and it stood off to the side in a sort of a "missing rider" tribute as
the casket was put in place next to the resting place of my mother,
Billye. A motorcycle's saddle had never before appeared more empty.

Big Red eventually became my own, or as "my own" as Big Jim's bike will ever be. I first checked with my siblings, many of them riders themselves, to see if any would object to me purchasing Big Red from Laura–I just wanted to see the bike stay within the family, and I would have been happy to see it go to any one of my brothers or sisters. No one objected to the transaction, and so Big Red came to live at my house where it has remained my go-to ride despite the fact that I have since gone through eight other motorcycles, each of which has played second-fiddle to Big Red.

Despite being *born* as a 1990 model, Big Red's story really began six years prior. In 1984, Mom had surprised Dad with a brand-new bright red Electra Glide, his first new Harley in a number of years. He and she rode that bike all over the country, often in the company of their friends on Honda Gold Wings or Suzuki Cavalcades, which were very fancy touring machines, loaded with every option, more so even than Dad's Harley. Dad and his friends loved to rib one another about their choice of motorcycles, each feeling that theirs was the superior *sickle*.

]

I provided Dad with what he felt was the "final word" on the matter when I penned for him the following:

> ### Rumbling Red
>
> *On a highway east of Vegas,*
> *One Friday afternoon,*
> *A dozen Honda Gold Wings*
> *Were whimpering up a tune;*
>
> *The riders all were comfy,*
> *All members of the club*
> *That bring along the kitchen sink*
> *And trailer out the tub!*
>
> *The computers set the air shocks,*
> *The speedo set on cruise;*
> *They play CDs or DVDs*
> *Whichever one they choose.*
>
> *Then, suddenly, VIBRATION!*
> *Their Wings began to shake!*
> *The trees began to quiver*
> *And the road began to quake!*
>
> *They saw it in their mirrors —*
> *A ruby-colored blur;*
> *They thought it was a comet*
> *But didn't know for sure.*
>
> *Then a glimpse of recognition*
> *As it pulled along the flank;*
> *And no one even had to read*
> *The logo on the tank.*
>
> *They knew that Harley "presence";*
> *They hoped the thing was fed —*
> *They thought to see a shaken man*
> *Astride the Rumblin' Red.*

But his footboards didn't shudder;
His windshield didn't dance;
His Harley smooth as velvet,
He gave them each a glance

And left them with the feeling
They had just beheld the king;
Though its seats are not reclining
And its dashboard doesn't ring.

Yes, the Honda's all were fancy
But they hadn't reached their goal;
For the Goldwing has the gadgets
But the Harley has the SOUL!

Dad memorized that poem and recited it around campfires or over dinner with his friends who rode the Japanese bikes.

When Dad decided to trade in "Rumblin' Red" in 1988, I matched the dealer's trade-in offer and became the bike's new owner, selling my BMW R100RT to make room in my garage. Dad's new bike was a fully-loaded burgundy and black Electra Glide Classic.

Shortly after I acquired "Rumblin' Red," I took off the large batwing front fairing with windshield and replaced it with a simpler old-school windshield from a police model, thereby creating a Sport model or *Road King* model years before Harley themselves offered this setup on their dressers. The photo below is of me and my daughter, Jill, heading out for the Grand Canyon on Rumblin' Red.

Dad and I took many trips together, he on his burgundy/black Hog and me on Rumblin' Red. However, Dad became a bit annoyed when it seemed that, at every gas stop, people gravitated to my bike and made comments on how nice it looked, overlooking his much fancier and newer model. I didn't realize how much this bothered him until he showed up one day on his brand-new, bright red 1990 Electra Glide Sport, the first year that Harley offered their big cruiser with the same windshield setup that I had fitted onto Rumblin' Red. With that move, Dad and I had nearly identical Harleys. And so "Big Red" came into our lives, a stable mate to Rumblin' Red.

This would be the last motorcycle that my mother, Billye, would ride on before she passed away in 1991. This would be the sickle that nearly took Dad to his own death when he crashed hard near Eloy, Arizona. After a major rebuild, this bike would carry Dad on many more adventures for another dozen years. In 2004, he and I, along with our wives, took these Harleys on what would be his final ride–a jaunt from Las Vegas to Independence Rock/Devils Gate, Wyoming. Dad was beginning to be confused about things as dementia became more obvious, and we finally had to hide his keys after this ride for fear he would go for a spin and not be able to find his way home.

For quite some time after Dad's passing, I kept Big Red just as Dad had left it, not wanting to alter a thing about his setup. Still – in the back of my mind, I dreamed of creating "the ultimate Jim Stephenson motorcycle"–a tribute bike that would pay homage to Dad and to all the motorcycles and adventures that had been a part of his remarkable life.

In 2014, I took a position with a company in Charlotte, North Carolina, and as the motorcycle transport company shipped Big Red to my new home in the east, a forklift operator crushed the front fender/wheel assembly of this treasured motorcycle. It was repairable, and they offered me a generous settlement of over three thousand dollars to cover the bike's injuries. This seemed like the perfect excuse to act on my vision of a tribute motorcycle.

I called my siblings and told them of my plans, fearing that I'd be expelled from the family if I made alterations to Big Red that made it "less Dad's motorcycle." With their blessings, I proceeded to strip Big Red down to the frame. It would reemerge as either a Frankenstein or a Phoenix.

All of Dad's past motorcycles, both those that I grew up on and those that I've seen only in faded photographs, tumbled through my mind. But the 1950s era struck me as the target of choice, the theme I was after. Here, I would find the right *flavor* in the motorcycles that launched Dad's lifelong passion for riding, and I studied his old photos, some of which are shown below.

For the color scheme, it seemed only right to keep with a red theme for Big Red, but rather than keeping with the more modern candy reds and metal flake treatments, I wanted the solid-body colors of the '50s. Mom and Dad's two-tone Duo Glide kept coming to the forefront:

Though the basic lines of the big Harleys have remained consistent over the years, there are a number of components that depart from what was found back in the day. Big Red's seat and saddlebags are styled differently than these old bikes, and modern Harleys feature a large rear truck that was not typically found on the older models. Rather than try to replicate the '50s paint schemes, I designed my own version, keeping the styling cues and paint colors true to the period.

I traded out the modern aluminum cast wheels that came stock on Big Red for chrome spokes and selected old-school wide whitewalls to call to the beholder's mind the age of sock-hops and drive-in theaters. I sought for, and found, badges and logos that were true to certain key years.

For the fuel tank, I chose the same Arrowhead badge (1959–1960) as seen on Mom and Dad's bike in the photo above, and for the saddlebags, I chose the Speedball tank emblems (1947–1950) which would have been on Dad's first new Harley. For the oil tank cover, I chose a graphic found on the earliest years of Harley's FLH line of motorcycles. To complement the rear of the TourPak (trunk), I chose a badge that is, admittedly, from the modern era, but it was the only one that looked right for this application, at least to my eye.

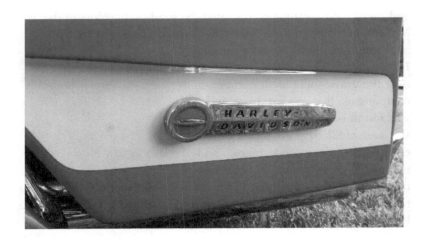

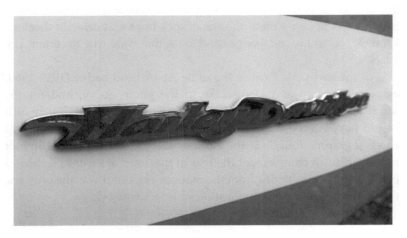

Dad claimed to be the first guy in Fayetteville, Arkansas (Dad's a Razorback) to fit white hand grips to his **Harley** (see the lower right photo of the four shots of his old bikes above). His friends all followed his lead to create a trend. I ordered in a set of "Coke Bottle" white grips designed for older bikes but not for this "newer" model, and I adapted them to work on Big Red. I also polished out the black nacelle cover around the gauges to more closely represent the aluminum nacelles of the '50s, but truly, Big Red's instruments are nothing like what was found on the old bikes, so I did the best I could. Over these gauges I hung a studded windshield bag like those found on Hogs from the '50s.

I replaced the modern "lollipop" rear turn signals with red bullet lights more correct to the period, but I kept the same fishtail exhaust pipes that Dad had fitted to Big Red shortly after he purchased the bike new. Finally, many Harleys from the '50s and '60s had windshields that were tinted in the lower half, often to match the color of the bike. Search as I might, no one made tinted shields to fit Big Red, so I had to create my own.

I spent a lot of time for many months working on Big Red alone in my garage, and I'll admit to talking out loud to Dad a time or two, asking what he thought about this idea or that. I never heard a reply, but I like to think he approved of the final product. When I revealed the motorcycle to my family, they all said I'd nailed it.

Shortly after completing the project, I entered Big Red into a local car and bike show in Charlotte just to see what unbiased judges might think–those who were not attached to the sentimental story behind the bike. To my surprise and delight, Big Red took home top honors at the show.

For now, Big Jim's Big Red continues life as my own time machine, connecting me with a past that extends before my birth. When I ride Big Red, I ride not only with my mom and dad–I ride with all the characters ever to occupy a place in Dad's stories. I ride with Bob Hunt, Gene Clampett, Bunkie Ramey, and Cheeseburger Smith. Each ride I take around the block is a winning ride up a mud hill climb in Arkansas or a jaunt below the border to Veracruz in Old Mexico.

This old stove continues to light new memories as my wife and I, my children and I, and even my grandchildren and I, continue to roll toward new experiences from the saddle of Big Red.

Here are two photos of a recent ride **across** the Mohawk Trail in New England with my oldest grandchild, **Carson**, who, remarkably, was born one day before the passing of his **great**-grandfather, Big Jim Stephenson (how's that for a passing of **the** torch?). Carson and I enjoyed a motorcycle adventure complete **with** campouts and downpours as the family tradition continues.

My two sons claim they have written up "joint custody" documents for Big Red in preparation for the time that I finally check out of this world, and it pleases me to think that Big Red will stir the hearts for future generations.

As for my own mortality, I've never been afraid to die, I've only been afraid not to really live, and motorcycling has played an enormous role in assuaging that concern. When my time does finally come, I've got a good idea what the next world will **look** like. When my time does finally come, I've got a good idea what the next world will look like and I wrote this poem in anticipation.

The Light Beyond the Grave

The last thing I remember,
That doctor wouldn't quit;
He pounded on my sternum
And cussed with every hit.

'Twas then I felt a numbness,
And a silence, oh, so still.
A darkness drew around me
Like a curtain 'cross the sill.

But with the blackness came a peace
That took away the fright;
  And as I wondered at the scene
  I saw that fabled light.

At first, so small, and far away...
But bright and white it grew;
With its approach a thunder rose,
A sound I somehow knew.

It came to me, and then it stopped;
  I squinted at the glare.
The light turned off, the thunder ceased,
And I could only stare

At the headlamp of a Harley,
With golden chrome so sweet,
As Dad, in bright white leathers,
Sat beaming on the seat.

  Amazed, I sought for answers;
I searched his eyes, he winked;
"Welcome, Son, I'll take you home.
" I stumbled back and blinked.

"Now, take it easy, Son," he warned,
"You know the Good Book said
  That, if you live a faithful life,
He'll reward you when you're dead.

"There's mansions many in His house,
Most find it quite the lodge;
He found for me the ideal room,
  I live in His garage!   "

Talk about your perfect shop -
My ratchet handle's pearled!
Any tool you name He's got;
After all, He built the world!"

  Dad fired up his golden Hog
And said, "Let's hit the skies!
I've resurrected Rumblin' Red
And now she REALLY flies!"

  I started toward the saddle
When something jerked me back;
My heart resumed its pumpin'
At the dang doctor's whack.

I coughed, I gagged, I tried to talk;
  I wanted just to die!
I faded off and dreamed for days
Of riding 'cross the sky.

But that was quite some time ago,
  And in this life you learn
To live each day your level best,
For death you wait your turn.

Now I am one of many who
Have viewed that awesome sight;
  At the portal of the grave
  I saw that shining light.

But only I have seen the source
Of the light that splits the fog;
Though few believe my simple tale
Of the angel on the Hog.

This concludes Molded on a Motorcycle, A Rider's Journey. Thank
you for accompanying me on the ride.

ACKNOWLEDGMENTS

The Stephenson dinner table has always been center stage for storytelling – it was so in my childhood; it was so when raising our own children; and it remains so today as grandkids join in on the tales of adventure, mischief, and hilarity. I first thank my parents, Jim and Billye Stephenson, for establishing this rich tradition. I thank my brothers Steve, Jeff, Scott, Monte, and Quinton and my sisters Shellye and Marcia for adding sharp wit and unique perspectives to this "Stephenson Stew" of shared anecdotes that so effectively cast a spotlight on the many joys of life. From this matchless seedbed, I have emerged a shameless storyteller who has picked up so much of value from each of my siblings.

A man could not ask for more supportive and inspiring children than what we have been blessed with. Jillian, Kimberly, Trent, Mitch, Rachel, and Audrey have, individually and as a group, pushed me to do what they feel I was made to do, to tell my stories to the world. I thank them for their encouragement and for demanding that I take action to write this book.

I express appreciation to my ever-enthusiastic editor, Stacey Smekofske, for her invaluable guidance on the road to publication. I extend deep gratitude to my riding buddy, Scott Doney, and to my niece, Andrea Stephenson, for providing insightful feedback as they pored through my rough draft. Their kindred spirits understood clearly what I was attempting to communicate.

More than anyone, my treasured wife, Donna, has been unwavering in her confidence in me and in her belief in the value of this project. Her insights as a voracious reader have helped me craft a far better book than I would have produced without her. She is my favorite riding partner, and I'm ever-grateful that she agreed to saddle up with me for this amazing and wondrous ride through life.

ABOUT THE AUTHOR

Wes Stephenson has swallowed more bugs than a swamp full of Louisiana bullfrogs, though, in his case, the ingestion was unintentional. After a lifetime on two wheels, with long-distance motorcycle riding being a primary interest, Wes's journeys have taken him to four continents and to every contiguous U.S. state to make rendezvous with more than just the occasional flying insects. Larger-than-life characters and unexpected encounters on the road feed into tales that are often humorous, sometimes hair-raising, and always quite entertaining.

A second-generation rider whose parents likewise explored North America from the saddle of their Harley in the 1950s, Wes has continued the tradition with his own children and grandchildren, who accompany him on rides across the countryside and campouts under the stars.

Wes has called many parts of the globe his home, including Saudi Arabia, Bahrain, South Africa, and seven U.S. states. His career in the automotive world has taken him from the grease racks of the service bays to a seat in the boardrooms of major national service chains. Wes and his wife, Donna, are the parents of six children and fifteen grandchildren.

Find more at WesStephenson.com

 facebook.com/Eversity.Publishing

Made in United States
Troutdale, OR
12/02/2023

15219529R00130